PRAYERS

FOR RECONCILIATION, RECOVERY AND RESTORATION

A personal journey for reconciliation with God through the Holy Spirit by the spoken Word

FEATURING FLESH CARDS

SHEILA RIVERA

SURELY
SAID
AND
SLEEP
HIS
FROM
AWOKE
JACOB
THEN

GENESIS 28:16

PRAYERS

for Reconciliation Recovery and Restoration

**A Personal Journey
For Reconciliation With God
Through The Holy Spirit
By The Spoken Word**

Sheila Rivera

Narrow Gate Recruiter Books
Fresno, TX

Publisher: Narrow Gate Recruiter Books
ISBN-13: 978-0615661353 (Custom Universal)
ISBN-10: 0615661351
BISAC: Self-Help / Twelve-Step Programs

Please contact administrator:
Sheila Rivera at
rivera.sheila@sbcglobal.net

FOREWORD

God needs you! Believe it!

He needs you just as you need Him!

He loves you so much and has a special assignment for you.

You are His special agent sent to uncover the lies that have been spoken over you-- lies about who God is and all that you are through His Son Jesus.

My prayer is that you will embark on your journey and embrace each opportunity, each choice and each assignment with the expectation that you are victorious as His daughter or son.

"If you abide in My word, you are My disciples indeed, and you shall know the truth, and the truth shall make you free." John 8:31-32 (NKJV)

Dedication

To my mother, Monette McDonald, who truly loved unconditionally and always had a heart for people. Her love has overcome many a foe and outlived the most persistent adversary! Throughout this writing the Holy Spirit would urge me to keep it simple for just plain folks!

A Backslider's Prayer

Sheila Rivera
July, 2008

My slumbering eyes awaken now anew,
Good morning Holy Spirit, I've missed you.

Great counsel in need, Your wisdom abounds,
You are beckoning me with groaning sounds.

You comfort me when I'm beyond remorse,
And hearken me to stay on eternity's course.

You lighten my load when the weight gets too great,
Lifting me gently to a more tranquil state.

You stick by my side though sometimes ignored,
Interceding as the living Spirit of the Lord.

My prayer for today and each day to come,
Is reserved, first-class seating for this Special One.

My temple prepared to receive and be true,
Good Morning Holy Spirit, I've missed you.

ENCOURAGEMENTS

God, whatever it takes, I am willing to do, to reach my freedom. –Debra

*If you want something that you've never had,
you have to do something you've never done.* –Nick

God didn't bring you this far to leave you. –Verenda

Did you pray about it? –Kim

Keep coming back. --Dunc

Walk by faith not by sight. 2 Corinthians 5:7 –Marchita

Integrity! –Marcelino

*F.A.I.T.H. For All Instances Trust Him.
(Heb 11:1; Prov 3-5-6, KJV)* –Marsha

Destination requires separation. –Jose

There's healing in the revealing. –Shirley

*May the Lord bless you and keep you, may the Lord's face shine
upon you and give you His peace. Num 6:24-26* –Catherine

*I can do all things through Christ who strengthens me.
Philippians 4:13* –Brenda

*There is no crop failure in Christ. (His Word accomplishes
what it was sent and meant for). Isaiah 55:11* –Kaye

You will never know GOD IS ALL YOU NEED until He is all you have.
–LaVera.

Fear not, lo, I am with you always. –Toni

*I am no longer a slave, but a child and an Heir.
Galatians 4:7* –Dennis

*You can look in the mirror, and that's what you and God
have to work with.* –Paul

Stay in the process. –Sheila

Prayer for Serenity

God, grant me the Serenity
to accept the things I cannot change.
The courage to change the things I can,
and the wisdom to know the difference.

Living one day at a time,
enjoying one moment at a time;
Accepting hardship as a pathway to peace;

Taking, as Jesus did, this sinful world as it is;
Not as I would have it;
Trusting that You will make all things right
if I surrender to Your will;

So that I may be reasonably happy in this life
and supremely happy with You forever in the next.

AMEN

Reinhold Niebuhr

CONTENTS

Let's Get This Party Started!

The angels are rejoicing in the presence of God over one repentant sinner. i In a like fashion, the Father is preparing a table for the return of His prodigal daughter/son; let us eat and be merry, for once I was dead, but now I live again.ii

Party Invitation

Father, I praise You and believe the only way for my sins to be forgiven is to admit I have sinned and turn from them. I lean on You, and believe that only Your blood is worthy of cleansing me. Most Holy Father, You sent Jesus to pay this debt for me through His death, burial and resurrection, and He is seated at Your right hand. Please accept this heart-felt invitation to be my Lord, my Christ and living King. Reside in me through Your Holy Spirit.

Lord, I am now washed into Your death with You. Just as You were raised from the dead by the glory of Your Father, I now arise and walk in the newness of my life through You. Accordingly, in the likeness of Your resurrection, my old man (old nature) was crucified with You, and that sin in my mortal body is done away with, and I will no longer be a slave to sin. I declare to have died to my selfish nature and lusts and I am free from sin through You.

Lord, You called me and tugged at my heart. You longed to hear me cry out to You and invite You into my life. You know me like no other, everything about me, even before I was born. Lord, I accept the invitation to dine with You and place You at the head of my table, my life. Be with me always as I embark on this journey known as life. Guide me, correct me, and lead me on a path that leads to You.

Lead me Holy Spirit on my trail of forgiveness. In Your perfect timing, show me those things I need to ask Your forgiveness for: _____

_____ .

Holy Spirit lead me to forgive others as readily as I have been forgiven: _____

_____ .

Help me to not yield to temptation, but delivery me from the evil one.

Blessed be God the Father of our Lord Jesus Christ! By His great mercy, His daughters and sons have been born anew to a life of hope through the resurrection of Jesus Christ from the dead, born to an unscathed, inviolate, unfading inheritance; kept in heaven. God offers protection to the faithful until the inherited salvation is revealed at the end of time. In Jesus' name I pray, AMEN!iii

---

i   Scriptural Reference: Acts 2:34-39 (NLT) Romans 6:3-7 (NKJV) 1 Peter 1:3-5 (MOFF)

ii   Luke 15:10 (WEY) 10 "I tell you that in the same way there is rejoicing in the presence of the angels of God over one repentant sinner."

iii   Luke 15:22-24 (ASV) 22 But the father said to his servants, Bring forth quickly the best robe, and put it on him; and put a ring on his hand, and shoes on his feet: 23 and bring the fatted calf, and kill it, and let us eat, and make merry: 24 for this my son was dead, and is alive again; he was lost, and is found. And they began to be merry.

INTRODUCTION

Provision is a matter of the heart. Delight yourself in the Lord and he will give you the desires of your heart.[i]

This introduction is a summary of the provision God made for the assignment of writing this book to bring Him glory.

My life was spiraling into a dismal abyss of destructive behaviors, self-loathing, and bitterness. . . In my journey to find peace and joy, I returned to my Creator and sought His guidance and advice. He has provided the people, opened the doors, and initiated the teaching and revelation to set this captive (me) free.

When I earnestly cried out for God's guidance in redirecting my path, He made all the supernatural connections that were needed in my life to regain a relationship with Jesus and ultimately with others. I have no doubt that this is His desire for anybody struggling with life's hurts, unhealthy habits, strongholds, hang-ups, and/or addictive behaviors. Provision, provision, provision!

God led me to a Friday night Lakewood Church Celebrate Recovery meeting. I had never heard of Celebrate Recovery, but I was free Friday night. I was separated at this time, not only from God, but my husband too. My husband would meet me there. This program, laced with God's victorious Word, laid a foundation for me to reconnect and restore many relationships. Provision, provision, provision!

Early in my recovery, I had a desire to help other people suffering and struggling with life choices causing guilt, pain, shame and condemnation--none of which are from God.

While attending a Joyce Meyer Conference, I was led to purchase a copy of WORDsearch8,[ii] a Bible software program with numerous interpretations of the Bible, Strong's concordance and much more. I was told by the clerk that this was the last copy. I felt so blessed to get the last copy, only to get home with it and feel overwhelmed. My feedback to God would be, "This is so over my head, what will I do with it?" Remember, I was reconnecting to the Word in my recovery and felt this was the Word on steroids! Provision, provision, provision!

A few months later, the Lord led me to The Prayer Institute at Windsor Village United Methodist Church with Pastor Suzette Caldwell,[iii] She taught classes on her book, *Praying to Change Your Life*,[iv] where I learned to pray in the manner as Jesus instructed His disciples when He said, "Pray like this."[v] We know The Lord's Prayer or what Pastor

---

i   Psalm 37:4 (KJV) " Delight thyself also in the LORD; and he shall give thee the desires of thine heart.

ii   http://www.wordsearchbible.com/

iii   *The Prayer Institute*, Pastor Suzette Caldwell, Houston, TX

iv   *Praying to Change Your Life*, Pastor Suzette T. Caldwell

v   Matthew 6:9 (AMP) "Pray, therefore, like this: Our Father Who is in heaven, hallowed (kept holy) be Your name.

Suzette Caldwell calls *The Model Prayer*. While in these prayer classes (101,102, and 103), the purpose of the WordSearch8 program became evident. I would diligently use it for my prayer writing assignments. Midway through my Prayer 102 class, the Holy Spirit gave me an assignment to write prayers for the Biblical steps in my recovery to profess God's victorious Word. No audible directive, no written agenda, just an overwhelming "aha, yes Lord," moment and vision that would put a fire under me to gain all I could from the classes. The life-changing revelations in His Word would fuel a fire for my enthusiasm. Through regular class attendance and fellowship, I experienced the power of His spoken Word. I fondly remember the first words from Pastor Suzette, as passed on to her by her own mother, "You can't put God in a box." Provision, provision, provision!

Then comes a connection at an Inspire Women's Conference[i] founded by Anita Carman, an organization who seeks to: *Develop women with the behaviors, responses and emotions that are fitting for a daughter of The King so that they can finish God's mission*. Provision, provision, provision.

Why do I tell you these stories, not to advertise any specific program or ministry, though I am ever so grateful to God for all of these, but only to show you that God's ways are not my ways. His thoughts are higher than my thoughts.[ii] I could have never orchestrated such a plan for my life. Each door that opened was filled with the incorruptible, indestructible seed of the ever-living Word of God.[iii]

You may be asking, why would she begin her book with this provision statement?

Simply to ask you the question, what are you needing today? I know someone who has all the resolve and all the truth to provide for your every need, JESUS!

My point? Small steps of faith lead to great leaps of provision!

–Sheila Rivera

---

[i] Inspire Women, Anita Carman, Houston, Texas

[ii] Isaiah 55:9 (AMP) "For as the heavens are higher than the earth, so are My ways higher than your ways and My thoughts than your thoughts."

[iii] John Osteen, Lakewood Church

SEEKING GOD'S PERFECT WILL 1

My journey on a road to recovery started by answering two simple questions, with two simple resolutions. Only then did I begin on my path of <u>ENLIGHTENMENT, ENTITLEMENT, and ENGAGEMENT</u> with the one and only Light of the World, Christ Jesus the Messiah, the Anointed One.[i]

1. Do I accept and profess Jesus as my Lord and Savior, my personal Higher Power, and am I willing to submit to His Authority?

2. Do I own a Bible that speaks to me at a level of my understanding?

A simple and humble beginning is exactly how Jesus came into the world to show me the Way, the Truth, and the Life.[ii] I am reminded when Mary, the mother of Jesus, early in His public ministry, sought her son to procure more wine for a wedding celebration in Cana. She gave the order to the servants, "Whatever He says to you, do it." His own mother knew the victory of submitting to His authority.[iii]

My journey will not be my way, nor my perceived truths, but the truth found in the infallible Word of God, the Bible. The result for my life has been a journey embarking on that perfect plan God has for me. You see, God knew me (just as he knows you) before I was formed in my mother's womb and my life is set apart.[iv] His plans for me are for good and not evil to give me a future and a hope.[v]

I had been captive and conformed to the ways of the world, and to pleasing my sinful nature, that is, my flesh.[vi] My life revolved around character distortions which had been formed from hurts and covered up with unhealthy, sinful habits. These character distortions culminated in self-gratification and self-edification. I had perverted, twisted or made crooked the truth. In all actuality, I had little knowledge of God's truth for me in His Word. God states in His Word, "My people perish for the lack of knowledge"--specifically the knowledge of His Word and will for my life.[vii] I remember frantically looking for my Bible, only to find it under my bed covered with dust. In my back-sliding state, I had conveniently slid (or hid) my Bible in a dark inaccessible place.

Hold on, there was some Good News for me. Through the sacrifices of Jesus at the cross, ALL my iniquities, sin and character distortions have been forgiven, erased, and remembered no more.[viii] This is the beginning of what I like to call **ENLIGHTENMENT**--light being shed on my sinful nature

---

i   John 8:12 (AMP) Once more Jesus addressed the crowd. He said, I am the Light of the world. He who follows Me will not be walking in the dark, but will have the Light which is Life.

ii   John 14:6 (AMP) Jesus said to him, I am the Way and the Truth and the Life; no one comes to the Father except by (through) Me.

iii   John 2:5 (AMP) His mother said to the servants, Whatever He says to you, do it.

iv   Jeremiah 1:5 (AMP) Before I formed you in the womb I knew (and) approved of you (as My chosen instrument), and before you were born I separated and set you apart, consecrating you; (and) I appointed you as a prophet to the nations.

v   Jeremiah 29:11 (NLT) For I know the plans I have for you, says the Lord. They are plans for good and not for disaster, to give you a future and a hope.

vi   Romans 12:2 (MSG) Don't become so well-adjusted to your culture that you fit into it without even thinking. Instead, fix your attention on God. You'll be changed from the inside out. Readily recognize what he wants from you, and quickly respond to it. Unlike the culture around you, always dragging you down to its level of immaturity, God brings the best out of you, develops well-formed maturity in you.

vii   Hosea 4:6 (AMP) "My people are destroyed for lack of knowledge; because you [the priestly nation] have rejected knowledge, I will also reject you that you shall be no priest to Me; seeing you have forgotten the law of your God, I will also forget your children.

viii   Psalm 103:2-3 (AMP) 2 Bless (affectionately, gratefully praise) the Lord, O my soul, and forget not (one of) all His benefits--3 Who forgives (everyone of) all your iniquities, Who heals (each one of) all you diseases.

(or flesh) by the good and Holy nature of God (Spirit). Jesus is the Light of the World. With the acceptance of Christ, I am now a light in the world.

I am moved by the invention of the solar-powered MP3 players which are used to bring the Gospel to the most remote parts of the world. What a remarkable innovation, God using his own created light source, the sun! I think of God's perfect timing for this enlightenment, for all the nations to hear the Gospel.

Enlightenment of good and evil and their sources and beginnings played an important role for me to realize the battle was not with flesh and blood (other people), but a spiritual battle.[i] The enemy, Satan, wanted to keep me preoccupied with my sin, instead of the fact that my sin debt had been PAID IN FULL by the blood of Jesus. This would be what the enemy would use to keep me bound with feelings of guilt, self-condemnation, and self-loathing. He used this to drain me of strength, to keep my focus off the real battle, my flesh! My sins are forgiven and remembered no more. I needed to focus on standing against my day to day, moment to moment, flesh-driven, carnal nature. It would be my Friend, the Holy Spirit, who goes hand-in-hand with me on this road trip.

ENTITLEMENT involved me coming to know and believe in my heart who God is, and who God says I am through His one and only Son, Jesus.

God is Holy, He is the King of kings, and Lord of lords. As a resident, citizen, daughter (or son) of His kingdom, I am privy to all the promises of God. All the promises of God through Jesus for me are "Yes and Amen, for His glory!"[ii]

- My Almighty God
- My Creator
- My All Sufficient
- My Master, My Owner
- My Eternal, Unchanging (the same yesterday, today and forever)
- My Provider

- My Healer
- My Banner, My Victory
- My Sanctifier
- My Peace
- My Righteousness
- My Ever-Present, God With Me
- My Shepherd

The person who has seen Jesus, has seen the Father--He is in the Father and the Father is in Him![iii] God is love and sent Jesus to show us His love for us so that we may have life through Him.[iv]

The Holy Spirit descended like a dove upon Jesus after he was baptized by John the Baptist.[v] After Jesus was crucified and ascended to heaven, seated at the right hand of God, He sent the same Holy Spirit to all who believe in Him. The Holy Spirit lives in me, in my body--The Comforter, Counselor, Helper, Advocate, Intercessor, Strengthener, Standby.[vi] This Spirit of Truth will guide me into the

---

i   Ephesians 6:12 (GW) "This is not a wrestling match against a human opponent. We are wrestling with rulers, authorities, the powers who govern this world of darkness, and spiritual forces that control evil in the heavenly world.

ii   2 Corinthians 1:20 (NKJV) For all the promises of God in Him are Yes, and in Him Amen, to the glory of God through us.

iii John 14:9-10 (GW) "⁹Jesus replied, "I have been with all of you for a long time. Don't you know me yet, Philip? The person who has seen me has seen the Father. So how can you say, 'Show us the Father'? ¹⁰Don't you believe that I am in the Father and the Father is in me? What I'm telling you doesn't come from me. The Father, who lives in me, does what he wants.

iv 1 John 4:8-9 (GW) "⁸The person who doesn't love doesn't know God, because God is love.
     ⁹God has shown us his love by sending his only Son into the world so that we could have life through him.

v   Mark 1:10 (NLT) "¹⁰As Jesus came up out of the water, he saw the heavens splitting apart and the Holy Spirit descending on him like a dove.

vi John 16:7 (AMP) "⁷However, I am telling you nothing but the truth when I say it is profitable (good, expedient, advantageous) for you that I go away. Because if I do not go away, the Comforter (Counselor, Helper, Advocate, Intercessor, Strengthener, Standby) will not come to you [into close fellowship with you]; but if I go away, I will send Him to you [to be in close fellowship with you].

full Truth.[i] How awesome is God to send His Son as my mentor to show me step by step how it is done---Believe like this, choose this way, walk this way, pray like this, think like this, and live victorious like this!

I accepted an apprenticeship under the authority of God, My King, who is all He says He is, knowing I can ask Him for guidance in any area of my life, any challenge, any question, everything involving my mind, my will, my emotions, my Spirit, and my body-- what an awesome **ENGAGEMENT**!

Who the Bible says I am! (to name a few)

- God's Handiwork
- Confirmed Blameless
- Complete in Him
- Citizen with the Saints in the Household of God
- Salt of the Earth
- First Fruit
- Peculiar Person
- New Creature
- Apple of His Eye
- Holy and Blameless
- One in Christ
- Near to God

- Child of God
- More than a Conqueror
- Free from Condemnation
- Light of the World
- Righteousness of God
- Royal Priesthood
- Forgiven
- Ambassador
- Beloved
- Friend of God
- Justified
- Overcomer

I am fearfully and wonderfully made, in the image of God.ii I am an imitator of God, as His dear child.iii Now I want to make the representation clear of who and whose I am!

ENGAGEMENT -- For me, this took the form of a Christ-centered recovery program called Celebrate Recovery at Lakewood Church,[iv] regular church attendance, daily prayer and Bible reading/study. There is also a tour bus full of people who encouraged me, held me accountable, taught me and shared with me their own valuable life journeys. I must passionately insert here, that I could have never done it alone. Two are better than one, for if one falls, the other one can lift you up, but if you are alone, you have no one to lift you up.v

A popular verse I like to quote from Jeremiah 29:11 tells me that God has a plan for me to prosper to give me a hope and a future. But I cannot stop there, verses 12-14 tell me that "THEN" when I call upon Him and go and pray to Him, He will listen to me. When I seek Him with all my heart, I will find Him, and He will bring me back from my captivity.[vi]

---

i John 16:13 (AMP) "15But when He, the Spirit of Truth (the Truth-giving Spirit) comes, He will guide you into all the Truth (the whole, full Truth). For He will not speak His own message [on His own authority]; but He will tell whatever He hears [from the Father; He will give the message that has been given to Him], and He will announce and declare to you the things that are to come [that will happen in the future].

ii Psalm 139:14 (KJV) 14I will praise thee; for I am fearfully and wonderfully made: marvelous are thy works; and that my soul knoweth right well.

iii Ephesians 5:1 (NLT) 1Imitate God, therefore, in everything you do, because you are his dear children.

iv *Celebrate Recovery*, John Baker, A Purpose Driven Recovery Resource.

v Ecclesiastes 4:9-10 (AMP) 9Two are better than one, because they have a good [more satisfying] reward for their labor; 10For if they fall, the one will lift up his fellow.

vi Jeremiah 29:12-14 (NKJV) 12Then you will call upon Me and go and pray to Me, and I will listen to you. 13 And you will seek Me and find Me, when you search for Me with all your heart. 14 I will be found by you, says the LORD, and I will bring you back from your captivity; I will gather you from all the nations and from all the places where I have driven you, says the LORD, and I will bring you to the place from which I cause you to be carried away captive.

2 PRAYER STRUCTURE

The following prayers follow the format from the book by Pastor Suzette Caldwell, *Praying to Change Your Life*.[i] The paragraph components of the Lord's prayer (or Model Prayer) are broken down as follows (abbreviated from Matthew 6:9-13):

PARAGRAPH 1:   Intimate Praise and Worship with the Father
                 Our Father in heaven, Hallowed be Your name. (v. 9)

PARAGRAPH 2:   Praying God's Will
                 Your kingdom come. Your will be done On earth as it is in heaven. (v. 10)

PARAGRAPH 3:   Praying for Your Needs (Personalized)
                 Give us this day our daily bread. (v. 11)

PARAGRAPH 4:   Praying for Forgiveness of Self and Others
                 And forgive us our debts, As we forgive our debtors. (v. 12)

PARAGRAPH 5:   Praying for Protection
                 And do not lead us into temptation, But deliver us from the evil one. (v.13a)

PARAGRAPH 6:   Kingdom Praise and Worship
                 For Yours is the kingdom and the power and the glory forever. Amen. (v. 13b)

Paragraph 3 of any prayer can be adapted and personalized by you to meet your particular needs.

My recovery is truly a me and I-centered journey, in order to identify the things I need to change. Praying God's will for my life needed to become my God-centered discipline to allow Him to come alongside me and work with me and through me. A journey that would allow me to fill the emptiness, brokenness, and distortions with God's Living Word!

Read each pray aloud, so that God's Word resonates in your spirit, it comes out through your speech and enters your mind through your hearing. In doing so, you are writing these words on the tablet of your heart. Also, take time to meditate on each forgiveness portion of the prayer, so you may reflect and ask the Holy Spirit to reveal to you the people and events you need to write and speak in these sections. I once told my son that forgiving others was 99% of the battle, citing forgiveness as the very reason God sent His Son Jesus to save the world, so that we may be forgiven. "Father I forgive them," should be a resounding daily offering on every Christian's lips from every Christian's heart. Forgiveness is not only a choice, but a mandate from God the Father. I am reminded how Paul was bold in commanding Philemon (1:8-9), yet for love's sake, to offer forgiveness and welcome back Onesimus, who ran away as a slave, yet was welcomed home as a brother.

Apply the following to the forgiveness sections of each prayer: (Paragraph 4--Forgiveness of self: List any sins that you have committed). (Paragraph 4--Forgiveness of others: Take a moment and ask the Holy Spirit to show you names or faces of people that you may need to forgive). (As He shows you, say aloud, "I forgive name of person(s)." Now, trust the Lord to heal any wounds in your soul caused by unforgiveness). Used with permission from Daily Prayer Power Guide, The Prayer Institute.

Note: Paragraph 4, Forgiveness of Self and Others, appears as 2 paragraphs so that you may write in the spaces provided.

---

i   *Praying to Change Your Life*, Pastor Suzette Caldwell

As a person with the propensity to cover my pain with drugs and alcohol, my body is where the enemy made entry into my life. The drugs and alcohol had a blinding effect that caused my sinful nature to manifest in many areas of my life. In my drug seeking lifestyle, I would not only ingest anything offered me, but I would go anywhere and do things to get drugs and alcohol to cover my pain. My body was negotiable and insignificant in this quest. Few limits, laws, or morals, were acknowledged or respected.

The thief coming to kill, steal and destroy[i] was evident in his quest to destroy my body or kill me. In my addiction, the resolve of my body being the home for the Holy Spirit (my personal trainer sent by God), was unrecognizable to me. This was Satan's first assault to render me powerless. Recognizing the importance of my temple, my body, the Holy Spirit led me to this key prayer for recovery, My Body/God's Temple Prayer. It involves what the Word says about God's temple, my body and the Holy Place that it is.

Under the law, God was the architect of magnificent temples where He would meet and commune with His chosen people. With the destruction of these man-made temples, God made His new temple a God-made one, my body. How appropriate for His new covenant, through His only beloved Son, Jesus, that His intimacy with me is intensified, brought closer, with my body as the new covenant, new temple. Wow, again God's ways are so much higher than mine!

I am called to have the mind of Christ, and this is another area where the enemy tried to come in and steal my joy and peace. The cycle of condemnation and negative thinking would play havoc on not only my actions and ways of thinking, but even to the extent of physical illness. Hence, the My Thought Life/Mind of Christ Prayer.

---

i   John 10:10 (AMP) [10] The thief comes only in order to steal and kill and destroy. I came that they may have and enjoy life, and have it in abundance (to the full, till it overflows).

My Body/God's Temple

My Thought Life
Mind Of Christ Prayers

MY BODY/GOD'S TEMPLE

My Creator, My Father, I praise You as the Bread of Life, who offered Your body in my stead, and I will never forget Your merciful obedience. Abba Father, even the 30 pieces of silver Your life was valued at by Judas, brought glory when the potter's field was purchased as a resting place for strangers. Father, I thank You for making me so wonderfully complex and in Your own image! Your workmanship is marvelous—how well I know it. Father, You are the head of the church, which is Your body. You are the beginning, supreme over all who rise from the dead. You are the first in everything.

O Lord, I give You all the glory, honor and power, for You created me for Your pleasure. Jesus, through Your intercession to God the Father, I was given a Helper, the Holy Spirit, and He abides with me forever. I know the Spirit of Truth for He dwells with me and is in me. I know my body is the temple, the sanctuary, of the Holy Spirit who lives in me, whom I received from You. I am not my own. Dear God, You paid such a price for me, I will glorify You in my body and in my Spirit, which are Yours. Elohim, My Creator, You commanded the light to shine out of darkness, and the light has shined in my heart to give me the knowledge of Your majesty and glory through Your Son, Christ Jesus, my Messiah. I declare I possess this precious treasure, the divine Light of the Gospel in this earthen vessel of my body, that the excellency of power may be shown to be from God and not from myself. Lord, I offer You the necessary thing of abstinence from the false communion of idolatry (or little gods). I will not let sin rule in my mortal body, and I will not obey its lusts (or flesh). By Your mercies, I present my body as a living sacrifice, holy and acceptable unto You, which is my reasonable, logical service.

Holy Spirit help me to keep my feet clean and acknowledge always where I take my body, Your temple, to bring You glory. Search my heart and show me those things unbecoming to my body. Help me to never worship and place little gods and idols before You. Help me to always be teachable and not stiff-necked. Lead me to recognize the common ways of society that may cause me to stumble and shed light on them. Lead me to proceed with caution and moral reverence to the path that You have directed for my life; yet, proceed with boldness and certainty at the call of the Spirit.

Forgive me when I am not mindful of Your presence in me. Forgive me when I make exception or become complacent to anything that is not pleasing to the Holy Spirit. Forgive me when I take back ownership of my body, forgetting it was bought at such a precious price. Forgive me for anything that blocks, veils, and prevents the Light of the Gospel from shining forth through me. Forgive me for taking communion with anything other than Your Body and Your Blood. Holy Spirit bring to my remembrance those things I need to ask forgiveness for: _____ .

Father, I forgive anybody who tries to appeal to or tempt my sinful nature or flesh. I forgive others who try to teach me to take ownership of my body, forsaking the sacrifice of You at the cross for my body. Holy Spirit bring to my remembrance anybody I need to forgive: _____

_____ .

Help me to not yield to temptation, but delivery me from the evil one.

God, You put all things under Jesus' feet, and appointed Him the universal and supreme Head of the Church, which is His Body; the completeness of Him who everywhere fills the universe with Himself. Every house has its builder; but He who built everything is God. In His Son's name, Jesus, I pray, AMEN![i]

---

i   Scriptural References: Luke 22:19 (AMP) Matthew 27:7-10 (AMP)Genesis 1:27 (AMP) Psalm 139:14 (NLT) Colossians 1:18 (NLT)Revelation 4:11 (KJV),1 Corinthians 6:19-20 (NKJV)2 Corinthians 4:6-7 (KJV), Acts 15:28-29 (AMP) Romans 6:12 (NKJV)Romans 12:1 (KJV) Ephesians 1:22-23 (WEY) Hebrews 3:4 (NKJV)

Reflections and Written Meditations

My Counselor, Blessed

Father, Your plans stand firm forever. Your thoughts stand firm in every generation. I praise You as the one who formed my heart and understands everything I do. Father, You have done many miraculous things. You have made wonderful plans for me. No one compares to You! I tell others about Your miracles, which are more than I can count. Father, how great are your works! Your thoughts are very deep. Oh Glorious Father, for as the heavens are higher than the earth, so are Your ways higher than my ways, and Your thoughts higher than my thoughts. Father, You give me food and provision, as I revere and worship You. I praise You Father as You remember Your covenant with me forever and know it is imprinted on Your mind. Father, I know that You can do all things, and that no thought or purpose of Yours can be restrained or thwarted. Merciful Father, You see me and take knowledge of me, and I am a concern to You Who knows all, understands all, and remembers all.

Father, I declare the Word is very near me, in my mouth, in my mind. and in my heart, so that I can do it. When my feet are slipping, Your mercy, O Lord, continues to hold me up. I declare and establish that when I am worried about many things, Your assuring words soothe my soul. You will uncover the secrets of my heart, and You will test my wandering thoughts. If there is any way of sorrow in me, You will be my guide in the eternal way. I profess to overthrow arrogant 'reckonings,' and every stronghold that towers high in defiance of the knowledge of God, and carry off every thought captive, as if into slavery—into subjection to You Christ Jesus. Who can know the Lord's thoughts? Who knows enough to teach Him? But I understand these Spiritual things, because I have the mind of Christ.

Lord. help me to think of, and seek only, the good in others. Help me to think of disappointments as windows of opportunity for growth and enlightenment. Father lead me to trust wholeheartedly in Your ways versus my own limited understanding of any painful situation. Lord lead me to recognize every anointed and approved thought through the Holy Spirit and Your Word. Strengthen me to bind every negative thought at its inception. Lord, lead my thoughts and intentions along the path of spiritual training, being useful and of value in everything I do.

Lord, forgive me when I submit to the "old man" and his thoughts instead of trusting you to lead my life. Forgive me for thoughts of customs, traditions and wives-tales that are contrary to Your Word. Forgive me for prideful, self-centered, egotistical thoughts. Forgive me for critical thoughts of others. Wonderful Counselor, forgive me for revisiting and holding onto negative words spoken over me. Holy Spirit reveal what I need to ask forgiveness for: _____ .

Lord, I forgive others for vocalizing condemning negative thoughts over me. I forgive those around me for gossip, cursing, and all manner of negative speech. Holy Spirit show me who I need to forgive:_____ .

Lord, Help me to not yield to temptation, but deliver me from the evil one.

Lord God, the Alpha and the Omega, the Beginning and the End; The One Who is, Who was, and Who is to come, the Almighty, the Ruler of all. No eye has seen, no ear has heard, and no mind has imagined the things that God has prepared for those who love Him. God has revealed those things to us by his Spirit. The Spirit searches everything, especially the deep things of God. In Jesus name I pray, Amen! [i]

---

i   Scriptural Reference: Psalm 33:11, 15 (GW) Psalm 40:5 (GW) Psalm 92:5 (KJV) Isaiah 55:9 (AMP) Psalm 111:5 (AMP) Job 42:2 (AMP) Exodus 2:25 (AMP) Deuteronomy 30:14 (AMP) Psalm 94:18-19 (GW) Psalm 139:23-24 (BBE) 2 Corinthians 10:5 (WEY) Revelation 1:8 (AMP) 1 Corinthians 2:9-10 (GW) 1 Corinthians 2:16 (NLT)

Reflections and Written Meditations

My Prayers for Recovery 3

In writing these prayers, I trusted the Holy Spirit to lead me from glory to glory in the visions and scriptures. I sought God's Word along my journey in the Christ-centered Celebrate Recovery Program, adding fuel to the exiting fire of each lesson, each step, each principle. The power in His Word enlightens the promises for me and tells me who I am in Jesus, and it is that blessed place where Christ first knew me long ago. My journey has been a continuum of finding out who I am, as my beloved Savior Jesus has known me, as well as His plans for me... until that glorious day when I am united with Him in perfection.

"Confess your trespasses to one another, and pray for one another, that you may be healed. The effective, fervent prayer of a righteous man avails much."

–James 5:16 (NKJV)

Stepping Out Of My Denial

Abba Father, I praise You for You are the Way, the Truth, and the Life. Father You are my Teacher, sincere, and all that You profess to be. You cannot lie, and You show no partiality or bias towards anyone. Father, as a descendent of Abraham, I am encouraged by Your oath that You bless me. I take hold of Your blessings with confidence, as a sure and strong anchor for my life. I honor You as my High Priest who went behind the curtain on my behalf. Merciful Father, it is not of my own strength, but You Who is always capably at work in me, energizing and creating in me the power and desire, both to will and to work for Your good pleasure.

Lord, I know that nothing good lives within me, that is, in my flesh. I have the intention and urge to do what is right, but no power to carry it out. God, If I say, "I have never sinned," I in turn make You into a liar and Your Word is not in me. Now, Lord, I am taught to change the way I was living. The person I used to be will ruin me through desires that deceive me. However, I am taught to have a new attitude. I am also taught to become a new person created to be like You God, truly righteous and holy. So I now get rid of the lies. I speak the truth to everybody, because we are all members of the same body. Out of my darkness, a prisoner of misery, Lord, I cry out to You and You save me from my troubles. You brought me into the light, out of death's shadow, and broke my chains. Lord, You wipe out all that I have done wrong. You create a clean heart in me, Oh God, and renew a faithful spirit within me.

Lord, I thank You that I am no longer estranged from You. I trust You to bring back my health and heal my wounds. I chose to walk in Your light and turn from darkness, and I trust You to direct my steps. I trust You with the healing of any broken relationships in my life. Lord, help me to use communication with You as my first line of assault for any temptation or painful thought. Grant me the desire, Oh Lord, to wait on Your response. Thank you Lord for sticking by my side, closer than a brother, through this journey of healing and restoration.

Father, forgive me when I go and pick up the very thing I have released to you. Forgive me when I neglect to consult with You daily. Forgive me Lord for any feelings of doubt or anxiety, especially those thoughts of self-condemnation. Forgive me when I pass blame onto others. Holy Spirit bring to my mind those people and actions I need to ask forgiveness for:_____

_____ .

Father, I forgive so many who have held me down or aided in my sinful behaviors. I forgive those who have physically or emotionally abused me. I forgive those who have neglected me. I forgive those who have cast a glare of judgment upon me. I forgive those who have spoken words of condemnation and death over me. Holy Spirit bring to mind those I need to forgive: _____

_____ .

Lord, help me to not yield to temptation, but delivery me from the evil one.

Lord God, My Creator, You are great and greatly to be praised; You are to be feared above all gods. For all the gods of the people are idols, but You Lord made the heavens. Hallelujah! Praise God in His holy place. Praise Him in His mighty heavens. Praise Him for His mighty acts. Praise Him for His immense greatness. Let everything that breathes praise the Lord! Hallelujah! In Jesus' name I pray, AMEN![i]

Scriptural Reference: John 14:6 (ESV) Mark 12:14 (AMP) Hebrews 6:14 (GW) Hebrews 6:19-20 (GW) Philippians 2:13 (AMP) Romans 7:18 (AMP) 1 John 1:10 (GW) Ephesians 4:22-25 (GW) Psalm 107:10,13-14 (GW) Psalm 51:9-10 (GW) Jeremiah 30:17 (GW) Psalm 96:4-5 (NKJV) Psalm 150:1-2,6 (GW)

Reflections and Written Meditations

_____
_____
_____
_____
_____
_____
_____
_____
_____
_____
_____
_____
_____
_____
_____
_____
_____
_____
_____
_____
_____
_____
_____
_____
_____
_____

STEP 1: We admitted we were powerless over alcohol (addictions/behaviors)--that our lives had become unmanageable.[i]

PRINCIPLE 1: Realize I am not God. I admit that I am powerless to control my tendency to do the wrong thing and that my life is unmanageable.[ii]

> _"Happy are those who know they are spiritually poor." (Matthew 5:3)_

---

i   12- Steps reprinted with permission of Alcoholics Anonymous World Services, Inc. (AAWS).

ii   Eight Principles Based on the Beatitudes reprinted with permission of Zondervan.

Accepting My Powerlessness

Almighty Father, I stand astounded at the evidence of Your mighty power, majesty and magnificence. I praise You Father, for You are able to do exceedingly and abundantly above all I ask or think, according to the power that works in me, I will give You the glory forever and ever. Lord God my Banner, I thank You for the victory of new life which is my inheritance that cannot be destroyed or corrupted and cannot fade away. My inheritance is kept in heaven for me and I am guarded by Your power through faith in my salvation.

Lord, many evils have compassed me about; my iniquities have taken such hold of me that I am not able to look up. They are more than the hairs of my head, and my heart has failed me and forsaken me. Pity me, O Lord, for I am weak. Heal me, for my body is sick, and I am upset and disturbed. My mind is filled with apprehension and gloom. Lord, what I don't understand about myself is that I decide one way, but then I act another, doing things I absolutely despise. Father, I know I cannot serve two masters: for I will hate one and love the other, or I will keep to one and have no respect for the other. I cannot serve You Lord and myself. Jesus, I know I have no chance at all to pull it off myself, but I have every chance in the world trusting You to do it.

Lord, help me to seek and cling to that peaceful and tranquil state of powerlessness. Guide me to be still and know that You are God. I lift up my anxieties and fears to You daily as I seek Your face. Lord, lead me to plug into Your power source, trusting I can do all things through You who strengthens me. Help me to do things that reflect my powerlessness including praying, reading my Bible, and attending church. My pain is real, my life is unmanageable, and I realize I am not God.

Lord, forgive me when I try to take control over situations for my desired outcome and not Yours. Forgive me when I grow impatient and anxious waiting on You. Forgive me when self-condemnation overwhelms me. Forgive me for not trusting in Your strength for my hope and my future. Forgive me for any resentment I have allowed to enter in me. Holy Spirit forgive me for:

_____

_____ .

Lord, I forgive others for dredging up my pain, my story, and my recovery. I forgive others for the painful labels that keep me bound. I forgive those who have tried to put a wedge between me and You Lord. Holy Spirit, show me who I need to forgive: _____

_____ .

Help me to not yield to temptation, but deliver me from the evil one.

Oh God Almighty, You are the God of all gods, You are the Master of all masters, a God immense and powerful and awesome. You do not play favorites; You do not take bribes. You ride through the ancient heaven, the highest heaven. Listen! You make Your voice heard, Your powerful voice. It is to this voice I listen, and in Jesus' name I pray, AMEN![i]

---

i   **Scriptural Reference:** Luke 9:43 (AMP) Ephesians 3:20 (NKJV) 1 Peter 1:3-5 (GW) Psalm 40:12 (AMP) Psalm 6:2-3 (TLB) Romans 7:15 (MSG) Matthew 6:24 (BBE) Matthew 19:26 (MSG) Philippians 4:13 (NKJV) Deuteronomy 10:17 (MSG) Psalm 68:33 (GW)

Reflections and Written Meditations

_____
_____
_____
_____
_____
_____
_____
_____
_____
_____
_____
_____
_____
_____
_____
_____
_____
_____
_____
_____
_____
_____
_____
_____

STEP 1: We admitted we were powerless over alcohol (addictions/behaviors)--that our lives had become unmanageable.[i]

PRINCIPLE 1: Realize I am not God. I admit that I am powerless to control my tendency to do the wrong thing and that my life is unmanageable.[ii]

"Happy are those who know they are spiritually poor." (Matthew 5:3)

---

i   12- Steps reprinted with permission of Alcoholics Anonymous World Services, Inc. (AAWS).

ii   Eight Principles Based on the Beatitudes reprinted with permission of Zondervan.

Finding Hope In God's Will

Eternal Father, I bow to You in moral reverence, as I find hope in Your mercy and loving kindness. I praise You Father, for I am convinced that the good work You began in me will continue until the day of Your return; developing, perfecting and bringing me to full completion. Loving Father, my faith in You gives me confidence that what I hope for will actually happen, and assurance about those things I cannot see. Father, my hope is in You, and I am of good courage as You strengthen my heart. I praise You Father for revealing to me the magnificent mystery of You living in me, giving me the hope of glory.

Lord, my hope is attached to You and the expectancy of Your will for my life. I will be secure because there is hope, and I shall look about and rest in Your safety net. I decree that before the sun is up, my cry for help comes to Your ear; my hope is in Your Words. My steps are directed by You, Lord, even though I do not understand Your ways. You are my hiding place and my shield; I hope in Your Word. I know the thoughts and plans you have for me are for good and not evil, to give me hope and a future.

Father, help me to know that these light afflictions of life are but for a fleeting moment. Help me Father to see the lifeline of expectancy filled with all the promises in Your Word waiting for me to reel into my life. Lead me not to defer my hope to the systems of this world or to my own devices. Lord, my hope is in Your perfect plan and will for my life. Draw me close to You when I waver and stumble off this course. Funnel my emotions and energies to a place of meditation with You and in Your Word. Help me to confront every negative thought with a promise from Your Word.

Father, forgive me for feelings of defeat and dismay. Forgive me when disheartenment tries to shake the courage of my resolve. Forgive me when I turn to my own devices that have repeatedly led to a hopeless dead-end. Forgive me for expecting to find my hope in other people. Forgive me Lord when my heart aches as my hope falters. Forgive me when I fail to lift up all things to You in prayer. Holy Spirit show me the things I need to ask forgiveness for:_____

_____.

Father, I forgive those who speak words of condemnation over me and try to steer me into hopelessness. I forgive those whose pessimism is like a constant symbol clashing and clamoring. I forgive those who do not know me and offer only worldly advice or resolve. Holy Spirit reveal to me those circumstances and people I need to forgive: _____

_____.

Help me to not yield to temptation, but deliver me from the evil one.

You are the God of eternal life, the ever-truthful God, who cannot lie, who made the promise of eternal life before the world began. Almighty God it is Your Servant, Your Chosen, Your Beloved, adorned by Your Spirit who proclaims justice to the nations, and in His name will be the hope of all the world. He was honored with the Name above all names, Jesus, the Lamb of God, in whom I place my hope and prayers. AMEN![i]

---

[i] **Scriptural Reference:** Psalm 147:11 (AMP) Philippians 1:6 (AMP) Psalm 31:24 (KJV)Colossians 1:27 (GW) Hebrews 11:1 (NLT) Job 11:18 (KJV) Psalm 119:147 (BBE)Proverbs 20:24 (NLT) Psalm 119:114 (AMP) Jeremiah 29:11 (AMP) Titus 1:2 (AMP) Matthew 12:18,21 (NLT) Philippians 2:9 (GW)

Reflections and Written Meditations

_____

_____

_____

_____

_____

_____

_____

_____

_____

_____

_____

_____

_____

_____

_____

_____

_____

_____

_____

_____

_____

_____

_____

_____

_____

STEP 2: We came to believe that a power greater than ourselves could restore us to sanity. [i]

PRINCIPLE 2: Earnestly believe that God exists, that I matter to Him, and that He has the power to help me recovery. [ii]

"Happy are those who mourn, for they shall be comforted." (Matthew 5:4)

_____

i   12- Steps reprinted with permission of Alcoholics Anonymous World Services, Inc. (AAWS).

ii Eight Principles Based on the Beatitudes reprinted with permission of Zondervan.

SOUND CHOICES FOR MY SANITY

Counselor Father, I praise You for while I was still a sinner You sent Your Son to die for me. Father, You are my refuge and strength and always ready to help me in times of trouble. I praise You for You do not brush aside the bruised and hurt, and You do not disregard the small and insignificant. Instead, You steadily and firmly set all things right. I draw my strength through union with You, and I am strong in Your boundless might.

Even though my mind and my body may grow weak, Lord, You are my strength and all that I will ever need. Lord, I will live in Truth, as this brings You great joy and happiness. I decree that Your power creates within me the desire to do Your gracious will and also brings about the accomplishment of that desire. I declare I will not fall into the trap of fear, but I trust in You, Lord, and I am safe. You have not given me a spirit of fear, but of power and of love and of a sound mind. I will not let my emotions run away and destroy my bones, but rather I will have a sound mind, which will make my body whole.

Lord God Almighty, I thank You for the armor and the instructions for its use that You have given me in Your Word. I praise You for teaching me forgiveness and its requirement for my restoration. I will no longer listen to the lies of the accuser of the brethren. My ability to make sound decisions will not be based on my circumstances, but through my meditation with You and Your Word. Lord, I thank You for the gift of free will, and for creating me with a variety of emotions. My soul will wait in silence for You only; for my expectation is from You.

Father, forgive me for doing the same things over and over and expecting a different result. Forgive me for making decisions based on prior experiences and not the truth. Forgive me for being faint-hearted in Your ability to restore me to sanity. Forgive me when I listen to and entertain the lies of the accuser. Forgive me when I am at ease as the victim. Holy Spirit reveal those people and situations I need ask forgiveness for: _____

_____ .

Father, I forgive people who remind me of my past failures and shortcomings. I forgive anybody who is not willing to recognize the new creation I have become through You. I forgive anybody who tells me my relationship with You is not genuine. I forgive those who have and who still try to victimize me. Holy Spirit reveal to me who I need to forgive: _____

_____ .

Lord, help me to not yield to temptation, but deliver me from the evil one.

The life of every living thing and the breath of all mankind is in God's hand. Great and marvelous are His works, Oh Lord God Almighty! Righteous and true are Your ways. He is The King of kings! All the kings of the land shall give Him credit and praise Him, for they have heard of the promises from His mouth which were fulfilled. In Jesus' name I pray, AMEN![i]

---

[i]   **Scriptural reference:** Romans 5:8 (NLT) Psalm 46:1 (NLT) Isaiah 42:3 (MSG) Ephesians 6:10 (AMP) Psalm 73:26 (GNB) 3 John 1:4 (GW) Philippians 2:13 (WEY) Proverbs 29:25 (GW) 2 Timothy 1:7 (NKJV) Proverbs 14:30 (MSG) Job 12:10 (AMP) Psalm 62:5 (ASV) Revelation 15:3 (Montgomery NT) Psalm 138:4 (AMP)

Reflections and Written Meditations

_____

_____

_____

_____

_____

_____

_____

_____

_____

_____

_____

_____

_____

_____

_____

_____

_____

_____

_____

_____

_____

_____

_____

_____

_____

STEP 2: We came to believe that a power greater than ourselves could restore us to sanity. [i]

PRINCIPLE 2: Earnestly believe that God exists, that I matter to Him, and that He has the power to help me recovery. [ii]

"Happy are those who mourn, for they shall be comforted." (Matthew 5:4)

_____

i   12- Steps reprinted with permission of Alcoholics Anonymous World Services, Inc. (AAWS).

ii Eight Principles Based on the Beatitudes reprinted with permission of Zondervan.

My Focused Redirection

My Shepherd, My Father, I hand over my ways to You. I trust You will act on my behalf. You will make Your righteousness shine like a light, Your just cause like the noonday sun. Abba Father, I surrender to You, and wait patiently for You. I am one of Your sheep, named after You, and I make myself low and come to You in prayer, searching for You and turning from my sinful ways. Thank You for listening to me from heaven, overlooking my sin, and giving life to me again.

Jesus, I boldly profess with my mouth that You are Lord. I believe in my heart that God raised You from the dead, and I am saved. Lord, You are in me and I am a new creature; old things are passed away, and all things have become new. Lord I trust in You with all my heart. I do not lean on my own understanding. In all my ways I acknowledge You and You direct my path. I declare I have the mind of Christ, and do hold the thoughts, feelings and purposes of Your heart. Lord, lead me in Your truth and teach me because You are my God, my Savior. I wait all day long for you.

Lord, help me to be diligent in releasing everything to You, trusting You will make all things right. Help me to surrender daily to Your perfect will for my life. Help me Lord to repent and forgive rapidly. Lead me to not go to sleep with anger in my heart. Let the sun not set on my anger. Help me to recognize when I am leaning on my own limited understanding in my imaginations, thoughts, speech and actions. Remind me daily that I am in this world, but not of this world. Ignite in me a need for spiritual food daily, which is Your Word. Holy Spirit empower me not to be a complacent hearer of Your Word only, but also a doer of Your Word. Help me to prioritize my daily quiet time spent with you.

Forgive me for allowing little gods to creep into my life. Forgive me when my pride rises up in haste. Forgive me when my body is not offered as a holy and pleasing living sacrifice to You. Forgive me when I listen to or entertain the accuser of the brethren, challenging my salvation and faith in You. Forgive me when I do not encourage others. Forgive me when I do not apply Your Word to my daily walk. Forgive me for not readily hearkening to Your fatherly conviction, cautioning and instruction. Holy Spirit show me those ways and interactions I need to ask forgiveness for: _____

_____.

Father, I thank You for Your most precious gift of forgiveness. I choose to pray it forward. Father, I forgive others who invite me to affairs that do not bring honor to Your name. I forgive those who mock me for my choice to follow You. Holy Spirit reveal to me those I need to forgive: _____

_____.

Help me to not yield to temptation, but deliver me from the evil one.

God judges righteous people as well as wicked people, for there is a specific time for every activity and every work that is done. Mighty and marvelous are Your works, O Lord God the Omnipotent! Righteous and true are Your ways, O Sovereign One of the ages. You are the King of the nations! In Jesus' name I pray--Amen![i]

i   **Scriptural reference:** Psalm 37:5-7 (GW) 2 Chronicles 7:14 (BBE) Romans 10:9 (BBE) Proverbs 3:5-6 (NKJV) 1 Corinthians 2:16 (AMP) Psalm 25:5 (GW) Ecclesiastes 3:17 (GW) Revelation 15:3 (AMP) 2 Cor 5:17 (KJV)

Reflections and Written Meditations

_____
_____
_____
_____
_____
_____
_____
_____
_____
_____
_____
_____
_____
_____
_____
_____
_____
_____
_____
_____
_____
_____
_____
_____
_____
_____
_____
_____
_____

STEP 3: We made a decision to turn our will and our lives over to the care of God. [i]

PRINCIPLE 3: Consciously choose to commit all my life and will to Christ's care and control. [ii]

"Happy are the meek." (Matthew 5:5)

---

i   12- Steps reprinted with permission of Alcoholics Anonymous World Services, Inc. (AAWS).

ii Eight Principles Based on the Beatitudes reprinted with permission of Zondervan.

MY DAILY SURRENDER

My Teacher, Abba Father, I am thankful that You stood at the door and knocked. When I heard Your voice and opened the door , You came in and had dinner with me. Father, You called me according to Your plan, and I love You. I know all things work together for good for me. Your action to take away my sins by Your death, burial and resurrection was predicted by You. I will cherish Your willful obedience forever. Dear Father, You have chosen me to be a special person to You, and I am holy and set apart from all people on the face of the earth. Father, You cause me to hear Your loving-kindness in the morning, and I trust You. You cause me to know the way in which I should walk, and I lift up my soul to You.

Jesus, I declare that You are Lord, and Your Father God brought You back to life. I receive God's approval and by my declaration of faith I am saved. I am not ashamed of You, Jesus. You are my chosen and assigned portion, my cup. You hold and maintain my destiny. I trust You to teach me how to live to please You, because You are my God. Lead me by Your blessed Spirit into clear and level pastureland. I listen for Your voice in everything I do and everywhere I go. You are the One who keeps me on track. I will not boast or be prideful, or let arrogant words come out of my mouth. You are the Lord God of knowledge and my actions are weighed by You.

Lord, help me to take the action of surrendering daily to Your will, living one day at a time and one moment at a time, trusting You always. Lord, Help me to not to look back or dwell on my past shortcomings and failures. Help me to believe in my heart that only You can make all things new. Lead me to abandon my old ways of reasoning, questioning, and playing out situations. Convict me in my heart that my first mode of action should always be submission, consultation and guidance from You. Father, instruct me with revelation of Your will for me in Your Word.

Lord, forgive me for complacency, slothfulness, and rebellion in turning things over to You readily. Forgive me Lord for anything done in private that does not please You, knowing you see all things. Forgive me when I put time constraints or expectations on Your response to my requests. Holy Spirit bring to my mind those things I need to ask forgiveness for: _____

_____ .

Lord, I forgive others for their unkind words or actions readily. I forgive others who are unwilling to hear and receive the Good News of Your saving grace. I forgive those who try to lead me off of the path I have chosen to seek Your will. Holy Spirit lead me to forgive: _____

_____ .

Help me to not yield to temptation, but delivery me from the evil one.

The Lord God triumphantly walks in the midst of the camp to deliver and give up the enemies. Therefore, shall the camp be holy, that He may see nothing indecent and turn away. Glory to God singing, HOLY, HOLY, HOLY, Lord God Almighty, Sovereign-Strong, who was, who is and who is to come! In Jesus' name I pray, Amen![i]

---

i   **Scriptural References:** Revelation 3:20 (AMP) Romans 8:28 (GW) 1 Corinthians 15:2-4 (GW) Deuteronomy 7:6 Psalm 143:8 (NKJV) (AMP) Romans 10:9-11 (GW) Psalm 16:5 (AMP) Psalm 143:10 (MSG) Proverbs 3:6 (MSG) 1 Samuel 2:3 (NKJV) Deuteronomy 23:14 (AMP) Revelation 4:8 (GW)

Reflections and Written Meditations

_____
_____
_____
_____
_____
_____
_____
_____
_____
_____
_____
_____
_____
_____
_____
_____
_____
_____
_____
_____
_____
_____
_____
_____
_____
_____
_____
_____

STEP 3: We made a decision to turn our will and our lives over to the care of God. [i]

PRINCIPLE 3: Consciously choose to commit all my life and will to Christ's care and control. [ii]

"Happy are the meek." (Matthew 5:5)

---

i   12- Steps reprinted with permission of Alcoholics Anonymous World Services, Inc. (AAWS).

ii   Eight Principles Based on the Beatitudes reprinted with permission of Zondervan.

TRUSTING MY SPONSOR/SUPPORT TEAM

Victorious Father, I praise You for the handpicked twelve apostles who came alongside You to minister with You. As a group, You and Your disciples came together and were constantly united in prayer. How wonderful that You led Your so-called inner circle of Peter, and brothers James and John up on a mountain alone with You to reveal Your glorious transformation and revelation as the Son of Man. In Your hometown of Nazareth, You called on the twelve apostles and sent them out two by two, and gave them authority over evil spirits.

You instruct me Lord that two people are better than one, and I declare we have a good reward for our hard work. If I fall, the other can help me get up. I admit that though one person may overpower me by myself, the two of us can resist one opponent. A triple-braided rope, or third person, will not easily be broken. When two of us get together on anything at all on earth and make a prayer of it, You my Father in heaven, go into action for me. When two or three of us are together because of You, I know assuredly that You will be there. As iron sharpens iron, so my fellow believers in You sharpen me.

Dear Lord, I trust You to open the doors and give me boldness to converse with others and seek out those You would put in my path who would be willing to listen and encourage me along my journey. Help me to put aside any shame or guilt in doing so. Lord, place people in my path who earnestly strive to live by Your Word and are willing to share their similar victories with me. Give me wisdom to rely on You first and open up to my earthly support team You have helped me formulate.

Lord, forgive me when I do not reach out to You, to my sponsor, to my accountability partner, or to my support team. Forgive me when I do not pray and read my Bible daily. Forgive me for contacting my team after the fact, instead of when it was a temptation. Forgive me Father when I try to make a sponsor fulfill other relationships in my life. Holy Spirit lead me to write down those things I need ask forgiveness for: _____

_____.

Lord, I forgive anybody who tries to discourage me away from my newly formed relationships with others who will support me. I forgive anybody who hurtfully tries to bring up my past and announce my sinful nature. I forgive those who do not readily recognize my newness in Christ Jesus. Holy Spirit, lead me to write down the names of those who I need to forgive: _____

_____.

Help me to not yield to temptation, but delivery me from the evil one.

At God's instruction, Moses held the staff given to him by God atop the hill in battle, and his arms grew heavy and weary. Aaron and Hur sat Moses on the rock, and by his side, each one held up Moses hand in support until sunset. In doing so the battle was won. Moses built an alter to Jehovah-Nissi, The Lord is My Banner! God will protect His chosen from one generation to the next! In Jesus name I pray, Amen![i]

---

i   **Scriptural references:** Acts 1:13-14 (NLT) Matthew 17:1-9 (NLT) Mark 6:7 (GW) Ecclesiastes 4:9-12 (GW) Matthew 18:19-20 (MSG) Proverbs 27:17 (NLT) Exodus 17:8-16 (GW)

Reflections and Written Meditations

STEP 4: We made a searching and fearless moral inventory of ourselves.[i]

PRINCIPLE 4: Openly examine and confess my faults to myself, to God and to someone I trust.[ii]

"Happy are the pure in heart." (Matthew 5:8)

i 12- Steps reprinted with permission of Alcoholics Anonymous World Services, Inc. (AAWS).

ii Eight Principles Based on the Beatitudes reprinted with permission of Zondervan.

WRITING MY MORAL INVENTORY

Ever-Present Father, I come to You to discuss my life. Though my sins are bright red, You make them white as snow. Though they are dark red, You make them white as wool. Merciful Father, search me thoroughly and know my heart! Try me and know my thoughts! See if there is any wicked or hurtful way in me and lead me in the way everlasting. You sought me when I was lost and strayed away, and You brought me safely home again. You bandaged me when I was injured and strengthened me when I was weak. I thank You Father for You are working in me, giving me the desire and the power to do that which pleases You.

Lord, I confess all my sins to You and stop hiding my guilt. I confess my rebellion to You Lord, and You forgive me. All my guilt is gone. I also confess my sins to another person and pray for others so that I am healed. My earnest prayers have great power and produce wonderful results. Lord, I confess my sins and You are faithful and just to forgive me of my sins and to cleanse me from all wrong-doing. Lord You have commanded me to be strong and of good courage. I will not be afraid, nor will I be dismayed, for You are with me wherever I go.

I thank You Lord for Your step-by-step instructions to restore me to unity with You. In my obedience to You I will be healed, made whole and my joy and peace restored, renewed like never before. I trust You to be with me always as I search deep in my soul through the Spirit, to honestly expose the things in my heart You reveal to me. I will not fretfully proceed with the writing of my inventory, but rather with expectant anticipation as a victorious overcomer through Your guidance and strength.

Lord, forgive me for when I distort the truth and do not readily repent. Forgive me for procrastination and hesitation in writing and confessing. Forgive me for picking things back up that I have turned over to You. Forgive me for not seeking assistance from my support team when necessary. Holy Spirit, bring to my remembrance those people, places or situations I need to ask forgiveness for: _____

_____ .

Lord, I forgive anyone who has hurt me in my past, physically and/or emotionally. I forgive anyone for acts of neglect during my life. I forgive those who have spoken word curses over my life. I forgive others for their character distortions. Holy Spirit bring to remembrance those I need to forgive: _____

_____ .

Help me to not yield to temptation, but delivery me from the evil one.

Come back to God Almighty and He will rebuild your life. Clean house of everything evil. Greatness, power, splendor, glory, and majesty are Yours, LORD, because everything in heaven and on earth is Yours. The kingdom is Yours, LORD, and You are honored as head of all things. In the name of Jesus I pray, AMEN![i]

---

i **Scriptural Reference:** Isaiah 1:18 (GW)Psalm 139:23-24 (AMP) Ezekiel 34:16 (NLT) Philippians 2:13 (NLT)Psalm 32:5 (NLT)James 5:16 (NLT) 1 John 1:9 (NKJV)Joshua 1:9 (NKJV) Job 22:23 (MSG) 1 Chronicles 29:11 (GW)

Reflections and Written Meditations

_____
_____
_____
_____
_____
_____
_____
_____
_____
_____
_____
_____
_____
_____
_____
_____
_____
_____
_____
_____
_____
_____
_____
_____
_____
_____
_____
_____

STEP 4: We made a searching and fearless moral inventory of ourselves. [i]

PRINCIPLE 4: Openly examine and confess my faults to myself, to God and to someone I trust. [ii]

"Happy are the pure in heart." (Matthew 5:8)

_____

i   12- Steps reprinted with permission of Alcoholics Anonymous World Services, Inc. (AAWS).

ii Eight Principles Based on the Beatitudes reprinted with permission of Zondervan.

Confessing My Sins

Jubilant Father, I will not cover-up my sins and I will prosper. I confess them and forsake them and You show me mercy. I thank You Father, out of sheer generosity You put me in right standing with Yourself, in the form of a pure gift. You got me out of the mess I was in and restored me to where You always wanted me to be. You did this by means of Your Son, Jesus Christ.

Lord my Righteousness, You are faithful and reliable. I confess my sins, and You forgive them and cleanse me from everything I've done wrong. I cried out "Lord help me" when I was in trouble. You heard me and saved me from my distress. I proclaim You led me from the darkness and deepest gloom; You snapped my chains and freed me from bondage! I confessed all my sins to You and stopped trying to hide my guilt. I admit to myself, and confess my rebellion to You Lord. You forgive me and all my guilt is gone! I make it common practice to confess my sins to another person and we pray for each other, so that we can live together whole and healed. These prayers of the righteous are met with much power and mercy.

I thank You Lord that when I confess to myself, to You, and to someone I trust, this three-stranded cord is not easily broken. You are the one who cleanses me from all unrighteousness. Lord, take away all the pain associated with my sin and cover me with Your peace and grace. I know there is no sin too great for You to forgive Lord. I know that the tears I shed in this journey are rivers of living water. I believe and trust in You for taking away the burden of my sin -- forgiven and forgotten by Your precious blood at the cross. Make these words I confess the foundation of my testimony of Your unfailing love for me.

Lord, forgive me for any pain I have caused others by my evil deeds, my neglect, or my hurtful words. Forgive me for alliances I have made to bring down or criticize others. Forgive me for my words that do not edify others. Forgive me for my sinful choices that have led to consequences for my welfare and health. Forgive me for the homegrown masks of self-righteousness I have worn. Holy Spirit, please reveal to me anything I need ask Your forgiveness for: _____

_____.

Lord, I forgive everybody who has hurt me in my past. I forgive those who at present try to bind me. I forgive those unnamed and their painful deeds done against me. I forgive anybody who has been neglectful. Holy Spirit, reveal to me those people and actions I need to forgive: _____

_____.

Help me to not yield to temptation, but delivery me from the evil one.

I know that my Redeemer lives, and He will stand upon the earth at last. God loves righteousness and justice. His mercy fills the earth. All on earth shall fear the Lord. All who live in the world shall stand in awe of Him. He spoke, and it came into being. He gave the order, and there it stood. The heavens shall declare His righteousness; for God is judge Himself. In Jesus' name I pray, AMEN![i]

---

i   **Scriptural Reference:** Proverbs 28:13 (NKJV) Romans 3:24 (MSG) 1 John 1:9 (GW) Psalm 107:13-14 (NLT) Psalm 32:5 (NLT) James 5:16 (MSG) Job 19:25 (NLT) Psalm 33:5 (GW) Psalm 33:8-9 (GW) Psalm 50:6 (ASV)

Reflections and Written Meditations

_____

_____

_____

_____

_____

_____

_____

_____

_____

_____

_____

_____

_____

_____

_____

_____

_____

_____

_____

_____

_____

_____

_____

_____

_____

STEP 5: We admitted to God, to ourselves, and to another human being the exact nature of our wrongs. [i]

PRINCIPLE 4: Openly examine and confess my faults to myself, to God and to someone I trust. [ii]

"Happy are the pure in heart." (Matthew 5:8)

_____

i   12- Steps reprinted with permission of Alcoholics Anonymous World Services, Inc. (AAWS).

ii Eight Principles Based on the Beatitudes reprinted with permission of Zondervan.

MY COMMITTED REDIRECTION

Priestly Father, I praise You because all things are from You. Through Jesus I am reconciled to You and brought into harmony with the ministry of reconciliation, so that by word and deed I bring others into harmony with You. Thank you Father for Your commandments. I will continue to obey Your instructions and will abide in Your love and live on in it, just as Your Son obeyed Your commandments and lives on in love. Glorious Father, teach me to do Your will, because You are my God. Your good Spirit will lead me on level ground.

I commit everything I do to You Lord. I trust You and You help me. I will think clearly and exercise self-control. I look forward to the gracious salvation that will come when You, Jesus, are revealed to the world. Now that I know better, I profess I will live as Your obedient child. I declare I will not slip back into my old ways of living to satisfy my desires. Jesus my High Priest, I am no more defined by the world than You are defined by the world. You make me holy—consecrated—with the truth; Your Word is consecrating truth. In the same way God gave You a mission in the world, You give me a mission in the world. Oh, how I praise Your Holy Name.

Lord, help me to welcome with open arms every change You desire of me. As I humble myself before You, set my path, my direction, and my choices in my day-to-day living. Help me to replace every misguided way of thinking with Your Holy Word to strengthen me. Lord, You are my mission control center and I will wait on You for direction. Lord, lead me to fervently study Your Word and pray daily, so You may reveal to me Your many mysteries and wonders.

Lord, forgive me when I become complacent in good times. Forgive me when I boast or think I have mastered anything. Forgive me for not following You daily and making my relationship with You my priority. Forgive me for not continually asking You to search my heart and test me. Holy Spirit, reveal to me anything I need to ask Your forgiveness for: _____

_____ .

Lord I forgive others who try to lead me off Your path of righteousness. I forgive others who reject the newness in my life. I forgive anybody for feeling abandoned, as I walk closer to You. I forgive anybody who tries to manipulate or interfere with my peace and joy that comes from You. Holy Spirit, reveal to me those people and actions I need to forgive: _____

_____ ,

Help me to not yield to temptation, but delivery me from the evil one.

The works of God's hands are truth and justice; All His precepts are sure. They stand fast forever and ever, and are done in truth and uprightness. He has sent redemption to His people; He has commanded His covenant forever: Holy and awesome is His name. The moral reverence of the Lord is the beginning of wisdom; a good understanding have all those who do His commandments. His praise endures forever. God has given Him an exceptional honor— the name honored above all other names—so that at the name of Jesus everyone in heaven, on earth, and in the world below will kneel. AMEN![i]

---

i **Scriptural Reference:** 2 Corinthians 5:18 (AMP) John 15:10 (AMP) Psalm 143:10 (GW) Psalm 37:5 (NLT) 1 Peter 1:13-14 (NLT) John 17:16-18 (MSG) Psalm 111:7-10 (NKJV) Philippians 2:9-10 (GW)

Reflections and Written Meditations

_____
_____
_____
_____
_____
_____
_____
_____
_____
_____
_____
_____
_____
_____
_____
_____
_____
_____
_____
_____
_____
_____
_____
_____
_____
_____
_____
_____

STEP 6: We were entirely ready to have God remove all these defects of character. [i]

PRINCIPLE 5: Voluntarily submit to every change God wants to make in my life and humbly ask Him to remove my character defects. [ii]

"Happy are those whose greatest desire is to do what God requires." (Matthew 5:6)

_____

i   12- Steps reprinted with permission of Alcoholics Anonymous World Services, Inc. (AAWS).

ii   Eight Principles Based on the Beatitudes reprinted with permission of Zondervan.

MY VICTORY IN JESUS

My Banner, My Father, I come to You and praise Your name for Your Son, Jesus, who gives me victory over sin and the grave. Father, You give me victory over my enemies. Lord, You take pleasure in me. You adorn me with salvation. Thank You Father that I have won the battle against the world through my faith in You. I praise You that through all things, I have the overwhelming victory because You love me.

Glorious Father, I submit my body as a living sacrifice, holy and acceptable to You, which is my reasonable service. I declare I am not conformed to this world, but am transformed by the renewing of my mind. I am able to discern Your good and pleasing, perfect will for my life. Lord, in my heart I plan out my course, but You determine my steps. Lord, I humble myself before You, and You lift me up. Lord, You give me abundant grace, as I submit myself humbly to You. I resist the devil and he flees from me. I draw close to You God, and You draw close to me, as I clean up my life, and clear my mind.

Father, I come humbly to You now claiming victory in my life through Your Holy Spirit who lives in me. Continue to show me my character distortions. Change my way of thinking to Your perfect will for my life. I submit my character distortions to You Lord. Draw close to me each day of my journey. Lord, I rejoice in the process of steady progress versus perfection. I know the power to change requires humility. I humbly ask You, Lord, to remove all my shortcomings. As I draw close to You, Lord, strengthen me to resist the temptations of my flesh.

Lord, forgive me for my sins and trespasses against others this day and reveal to me those things I need to recognize as such. Forgive me for not celebrating the victories of others. Forgive me when pride or a sense of accomplishment, without You as the source, tries to rise up in me. Holy Spirit reveal to me those actions I need to ask forgiveness for: _____

_____ .

Your victory at the cross enables me to forgive others who try to steer me off Your victorious course. Holy Spirit reveal to me those people and situations I need to forgive: _____

_____ .

Help me to not yield to temptation, but delivery me from the evil one.

The Temple Gate belongs to God, so the victors can enter and praise. The Lord saves His anointed; He will answer him from His holy heaven with the saving strength of His right hand. From long ago, God has been King, the one who has been victorious throughout the earth. In Jesus name I pray, AMEN![i]

---

i **Scriptural Reference:** James 4:6-8, (NKJV), 1 Cor 15:57 (NLT), Psalm 44:7 (NLT), 1 John 5:4 (NLT) Rom 8:37 (NLT), Roman 12:1-3, Psalm 149:4 (NKJV), Proverbs 16:9 (NKJV), Psalm 118:20 (MSG), Psalm 20:6 (AMP). Psalm 74:12 (GW)

_____
_____
_____
_____
_____
_____
_____
_____
_____
_____
_____
_____
_____
_____
_____
_____
_____
_____
_____
_____
_____
_____
_____

STEP 6: We were entirely ready to have God remove all these defects of character. [i]

STEP 7: We humbly asked Him to remove our shortcomings. [i]

PRINCIPLE 5: Voluntarily submit to every change God wants to make in my life and humbly ask Him to remove my character defects. [ii]

> *"Happy are those whose greatest desire is to do what God requires." (Matthew 5:6)*

_____

i   12- Steps reprinted with permission of Alcoholics Anonymous World Services, Inc. (AAWS).

ii Eight Principles Based on the Beatitudes reprinted with permission of Zondervan.

Making Amends To Others

Healing Father, I thank You that I am called to freedom and do not let my freedom be an incentive to my flesh and an opportunity or excuse for selfishness, but through love I will serve others. For Your whole Law concerning human relationships is compiled within the one precept, I shall love my neighbors as myself. Lord, I go to my father in peace, and I will be buried in a good old age. I praise You Father, because the Spirit of the Lord anointed You to preach the gospel to the poor; You were sent to heal the brokenhearted, to preach deliverance to the captives, recovering sight to the blind, to set at liberty them that are bruised, and to announce the year of the Lord's favor.

As Your follower Lord, I treat others as I would like to be treated. I do not judge others, and Lord, You do not judge me, I do not condemn others and You do not condemn me. I forgive others and Lord, You forgive me. Lord, I am merciful and happy with joy and satisfaction in God's favor, regardless of my outward conditions, for I obtain mercy! I am a peacemaker and happy with joy and satisfaction in God's favor, regardless of my outward conditions, for I am called a child of God. I am not only concerned about my own interests, but I am also concerned about the interests of others.

Father, I humbly submit to You the names and situations of others I have hurt or who have hurt me. In like manner, Lord, I lean on Your Wisdom calling me to offer amends to those persons in a manner that will be pleasing to You, Father. Help me to stay focused on my part of any situation. Lord, I seek Your guidance for the perfect timing and opportunity to make amends. I release expectations of others to You, Lord prior to my making amends. I commit to lift up every situation to You in prayer. Lord, as my Prince of Peace, I trust You to calm all my emotions launched by re-visiting my inventory..

Father, forgive me for not praying for those who persecute me. Forgive me for procrastinating in writing and seeking Your will for my inventory and amends. Forgive me when I am quick to judge and criticize others. Holy Spirit, reveal to me those persons, places, or things I need to ask forgiveness for: _____

_____ .

Father, I forgive others quickly, and never hold a grudge. Forgive me for having selfish expectations of others. Holy Spirit, reveal to me those I need to forgive: _____

_____ .

Help me to not yield to temptation, Lord, but deliver me from the evil one.

GOD is my Refuge and Strength, a very present and well-proved help in trouble. Though the waters roar and foam, though the mountains tremble at its swelling and tumult, there is a river whose streams shall make glad the city of God, the holy place of the temple of the Most High. God is in the midst of the city and it shall not be moved: God shall protect the city from the early dawn. In the name of Jesus I pray, AMEN![i]

---

i **Scriptural Reference**: Galatians 5:13-14 (AMP) Genesis 15:15 (KJV) Luke 4:18-19 (KJV) Luke 1:76 (TLB) Luke 6:37 (AMP) Matthew 5:7 (AMP) Matthew 5:9 (AMP) Philippians 2:4 (GW) Psalm 46:1 (AMP) Psalm 46:3-5 (AMP)

_____
_____
_____
_____
_____
_____
_____
_____
_____
_____
_____
_____
_____
_____
_____
_____
_____
_____
_____
_____
_____
_____
_____
_____
_____
_____
_____

STEP 8: We made a list of all persons we had harmed, and became willing to make amends to them all. [i]

PRINCIPLE 6: Evaluate all my relationships. Offer forgiveness to those who have hurt me and make amends for harm I've done to others, except when to do so would harm them or others. [ii]

"Happy are the merciful." (Matthew 5:7)

"Happy are the peacemakers." (Matthew 5:9)

_____

i 12- Steps reprinted with permission of Alcoholics Anonymous World Services, Inc. (AAWS).

ii Eight Principles Based on the Beatitudes reprinted with permission of Zondervan.

Offering Forgiveness

Righteous Father, You were raised to life, and You saw no corruption. Thank You Father, I clearly know and understand that Your forgiveness and removal of sins is now proclaimed to me. Most gracious Father, I have my redemption through Your blood, and the forgiveness of my sins. You are the exact likeness of the unseen God; You are his Firstborn of all creation.

Lord, I love my enemies and do good to those who hate me. I bless and pray for those who curse me and those who abuse me. I will turn and offer the other cheek after being struck on one cheek. To the person who takes my outer garment, I will not withhold my undergarment. Merciful Father, I will give to every man that begs for necessities, and I will not ask for them back. I will do unto others, as I would like them to do unto me. I do not repay evil with evil. I am careful to do what is right in the eyes of everybody. I declare, if at all possible, as far as it depends on me, I will live at peace with everyone.

Lord, I humbly come to You knowing that I must forgive to be forgiven. Guide me through the years of hurts and entanglements that have led me astray from Your will for my life. Empower me to offer sincere forgiveness to those who have reckoned with me harshly and tried to destroy my very being. Jesus, may I lean on the rugged cross on which You so unfairly bore my transgressions and afflictions without hesitation or rebellion. Restore my joy and happiness by making me a merciful giver and a peacemaker.

Lord, forgive me when I am quick to see the sawdust in another's eye, when I have a log in my own. Forgive me when I judge and condemn others. Forgive me when I hold grudges. Father, forgive me when I do not try to keep the peace. Father, forgive me for not trusting You totally to the vengeance of my transgressors. Forgive me Lord, for thinking anyone is not worthy of Your forgiveness. Holy Spirit reveal those persons, places, or things I need to ask forgiveness for: _____

_____ .

Father, help me to forgive others quickly, and never hold a grudge or pass judgment on others. Holy Spirit, reveal those persons, places, or things I need to forgive:_____

_____ .

Help me to not yield to temptation, but deliver me from the evil one.

All are justified and made in right standing with You God, freely and gratuitously by Your grace, through the redemption which is provided in Your Son, Christ Jesus; Who, You put forward before the eyes of all as a mercy seat by His blood, the cleansing and life-giving sacrifice of atonement and reconciliation, to be received through faith. This was to show Your righteousness, because in Your divine bloodline, You passed over and ignored former sins without punishment. In the forgiving and atoning Blood and Name of Jesus I pray, Amen![i]

---

i   **Scriptural Reference:** Romans 3:24-25 (AMP) Matthew 5:7-9 (KJV) Matthew 7:3-4 (KJV)Romans 12:17-18 (KJV) Luke 6:27-31 (KJV) Colossians 1:14-15 (AMP) Acts 13:37-39 (AMP)

Reflections and Written Meditations

_____
_____
_____
_____
_____
_____
_____
_____
_____
_____
_____
_____
_____
_____
_____
_____
_____
_____
_____
_____
_____
_____
_____

STEP 8: We made a list of all persons we had harmed, and became willing to make amends to them all. [i]

STEP 9: We made direct amends to such people wherever possible, except when to do so would injure them or others. [i]

PRINCIPLE 6: Evaluate all my relationships. Offer forgiveness to those who have hurt me and make amends for harm I've done to others, except when to do so would harm them or others. [ii]

"Happy are the merciful." (Matthew 5:7)

"Happy are the peacemakers." (Matthew 5:9)

---

i   12- Steps reprinted with permission of Alcoholics Anonymous World Services, Inc. (AAWS).

ii   Eight Principles Based on the Beatitudes reprinted with permission of Zondervan.

GOD'S GRACE IS ENOUGH

Gracious Father, You are my Great High Priest, who has departed into the heavens, You are the Son of God, let me hold fast my profession. Thank You Father, for You are not a high priest who cannot be touched with the feeling of my infirmities; but You were in all points tempted like I was, yet without sin. Let me therefore come boldly unto Your throne of grace, so that I may obtain mercy, and find grace to help in time of need. Father, in You I have redemption through Your blood, the forgiveness of sins, according to the riches of Your grace.

I brace up my mind; I am sober and alert. I set my hope wholly and unchangeably on the divine favor that is coming to me when You Lord are revealed. I am saved by grace through faith; and my salvation is not of my own doing, but it is a gift from You God. This is not the result of anything I can do, so that I cannot boast or take glory for myself. I have been crucified with Christ and I no longer live, but Christ lives in me; and the life I now live in this body I live by faith and complete trust in the Son of God, who loved me and gave Himself up for me. Therefore, I do not treat God's gracious gift as something of minor importance and defeat its very purpose. For if justification and righteousness came through observing the Law, then Christ died for no purpose and in vain.

Help me Lord, to savor this most precious gift You have given me. Help me to love others in their unlovable state, just as You loved me. Help me to ever so diligently evaluate my relationships, forgive others who have hurt me, and make amends for harm I have done to others. Help me Lord to model Your grace as it was freely given. Help me to not to expect anything in return. Help me to not to quarrel with anyone, but be at peace with everyone, as much as is possible. Help me Father to not be proud or boastful in any service to You and others.

Lord, forgive me when I find no compassion for others while they are still sinning. Forgive me when I forsake Your name. Forgive me Father, when I pick quarrels with others. In this moment of silence, Holy Spirit, reveal to me those people, places and things, I need to ask Your forgiveness for: _____

_____ .

Father, help me to forgive others quickly. I forgive readily others struggling with painful situations in their life, recognizing their actions as an outcry for Your love and grace. Holy Spirit reveal to me those persons or situations I need to forgive: _____

_____ .

Help me to not yield to temptation, but deliver me from the evil one.

Lord God, You are my Sun and Shield; Lord, You bestow present grace and favor, and future glory! The Lord is gracious and full of compassion, slow to anger and abounding in mercy and loving-kindness. He has made His wonderful works to be remembered; the Lord is gracious, merciful and full of loving compassion. In the name of Jesus I pray, Amen![i]

---

i   Scriptural references: Hebrews 4:14-16 (KJV) Ephesians 1:7 (KJV) Ephesians 2:8-9 (AMP) 1 Peter 1:13 (AMP) Galatians 2:20-21 (AMP)
     Psalm 84:11-12 (AMP), Psalm 145:8 (AMP) Psalm 111:4 (AMP)

Reflections and Written Meditations

_____
_____
_____
_____
_____
_____
_____
_____
_____
_____
_____
_____
_____
_____
_____
_____
_____
_____
_____
_____
_____
_____
_____
_____
_____
_____

STEP 9: We made direct amends to such people wherever possible, except when to do so would injure them or others. [i]

PRINCIPLE 6: Evaluate all my relationships. Offer forgiveness to those who have hurt me and make amends for harm I've done to others, except when to do so would harm them or others. [ii]

"Happy are the merciful." (Matthew 5:7)

"Happy are the peacemakers." (Matthew 5:9)

---

i   12- Steps reprinted with permission of Alcoholics Anonymous World Services, Inc. (AAWS).

ii   Eight Principles Based on the Beatitudes reprinted with permission of Zondervan.

Continuing In Truth

Wonderful Father, my Lord Jesus Christ, the source of every mercy and the One who comforts, consoles, and encourages me. Father, You comfort me in every trouble and hardship, so that I may also be able to comfort, console, and encourage others in trouble or distress, with the same help and comfort which You have given me. Father, I dwell in the secret place of the Most High and shall remain stable and fixed under the shadow of the Almighty, whose power no foe can withstand. I say of You, Father, You are my Refuge and my Fortress, my God; on You I lean and rely, and in You I confidently trust!

I believe in you Jesus. I abide in Your Word and hold fast to Your teachings and live in accordance with them, and I am truly Your disciple. I commit to know the Truth, and the Truth has set me free. If I say I have no sin, refusing to admit that I am a sinner, then I delude and lead myself astray, and the Truth which the Gospel represents does not dwell in my heart. I freely admit that I have sinned and confess my sins, and You are faithful and just and forgive me my sins and cleanse me from all unrighteousness. I declare I will let the Word of Christ dwell in me richly in all Wisdom; teaching and admonishing others in psalms and hymns and spiritual songs, singing with grace in my heart to You Lord.

Lord, help me to treat everyone equally with love and understanding. Help me to never forget Your abounding grace that has brought me thus far. Let me use this same grace to serve as the catalyst for me to help others. Help me to love the unlovable, just as You have loved me. Help me to humbly submit to Your will, striving ever diligently, yet never being boastful or proud. Give me boldness to profess You as the only true High and Mighty God. Help me, Lord, to walk in Truth and Wisdom, accessible to me through Your sacred Word.

Father, forgive me when I brag and am boastful and rob You of Your glory. Forgive me when I hold a grudge and attempt to enter Your secret place. Forgive me for not submitting to Your examination and testing of my ways, and neglecting to honestly abide by Your standards You have set for me in Your Word. Holy Spirit bring to my mind those circumstances I need to ask forgiveness for:

_____ .

Father, I forgive those who have repeatedly tried to lead me astray from my walk with You in words or deeds. Holy Spirit bring to mind those I need to forgive: _____

_____ .

Help me to not yield to temptation, Lord, but deliver me from the evil one.

Great is Your goodness, which You have laid up for those who fear, revere, and worship You, goodness which You have wrought for those who trust and take refuge in You before the sons of men! In the secret place of Your presence, You hide Your flock from the plots of men; You keep Your sheep secretly in a shelter, safe from the quarrelsome tongues. Blessed be the Lord! For He has shown His people His marvelous mercy in a city under attack. In Jesus' name I pray, Amen![i]

---

i   Scriptural References: 2 Corinthians 1:3-4 (AMP) Psalm 91:1-2 (AMP) John 8:31-32 (AMP) 1 John 1:8-10 (AMP) Colossians 3:16 (KJV) Psalm 31:19-21 (AMP/GW)

Reflections and Written Meditations

_____
_____
_____
_____
_____
_____
_____
_____
_____
_____
_____
_____
_____
_____
_____
_____
_____
_____
_____
_____
_____
_____
_____
_____
_____

STEP 10: We continued to take personal inventory and when we were wrong promptly admitted it. [i]

PRINCIPLE 7: Reserve a daily time with God for self-examination, Bible reading, and prayer in order to know God and His will for my life and to gain the power to follow His will. [ii]

"Happy are those who are persecuted because they do what God requires." (Matthew 5:10)

_____

i   12- Steps reprinted with permission of Alcoholics Anonymous World Services, Inc. (AAWS).

ii Eight Principles Based on the Beatitudes reprinted with permission of Zondervan.

TAKING DAILY INVENTORY

High Priest, My Father, I thank You because the works of Your hands are absolute truth and justice, faithful and right; and all Your decrees and precepts are trustworthy. Father, You sent redemption to me; You commanded Your covenant to be forever; Holy is Your name, inspiring in me awe, reverence, and godly fear. Gracious Father, my reverent fear and worship of You is the beginning of Wisdom. You lead me as I practice this, to have a good understanding to do Your Will. Your praise endures forever!

Lord, the fruit of the Holy Spirit dwells in me, and I shall walk in love, joy, peace, patience, kindness, goodness, and faithfulness. I exhibit gentleness, humility and self-control. There is no law against these fruits. I belong to You Jesus, and have crucified my flesh with its passions, appetites, and desires. I live with God in my life through the Holy Spirit. My conduct and walk is controlled by the Holy Spirit. I will not become self-conceited, competitive, challenging, or provoking and irritating to others. I will not become envious or jealous of others.

Lord, guide me to live humbly daily, in reality and not in denial. Keep me steadfast on my journey of applying the principles I have learned. Holy Spirit guide me as I make choices about the emotions that affect my thinking and actions. Lord, burnish in my heart the first and greatest commandment to, love You Lord, my God, with all my heart, soul and mind. Likewise, Your second commandment to love my neighbors as myself. Help these commandments to be at the center of all I do, so that my actions will be consistent with my words. Lord, help me to think before I speak, and have no worthless words come out of my mouth, but help me to speak good and beneficial words to the spiritual progress of others. Help me to use Your commandments and teachings as a daily checklist for self-reflection and self-examination, so that I gain power to do Your will. Lord, help me to make amends promptly and ask for forgiveness daily.

Today, Father, forgive me when I neglect and deprive my spirit of food, which is Your Holy Word. Forgive me for not showing love to others. Forgive me for losing patience and being quick to anger and speak unkindly. Forgive me for any unkind action or thought towards another. Holy Spirit bring to my mind those actions I need to ask Your forgiveness for: _____

_____ .

Today, in a like fashion, Lord, I forgive others promptly, and harbor no resentment or grudge. I release those names to You Lord in obedience to You. Holy Spirit bring to my mind those people I need to forgive: _____

_____ .

Help me to not yield to temptation, but deliver me from the evil one.

When the Son of Man comes in His glory and all His angels are with Him, He will sit on His glorious throne. God has a made a covenant with His people! He has put His law within us and written it on our hearts. He is our God and we are His people. In the name of Jesus' I pray, Amen![i]

---

i   Scriptural References: Psalm 111:7-10 (AMP/ESV) Galatians 5:22-26 (AMP) 2 Peter 1:6-8 (AMP) Matthew 25:31-34 (GW) Jer 31:33 (AMP)

_____
_____
_____
_____
_____
_____
_____
_____
_____
_____
_____
_____
_____
_____
_____
_____
_____
_____
_____
_____
_____
_____
_____
_____
_____
_____

STEP 10: We continued to take personal inventory and when we were wrong promptly admitted it. [i]

PRINCIPLE 7: Reserve a daily time with God for self-examination, Bible reading, and prayers in order to know God and His will for my life and to gain the power to follow His will. [ii]

"Happy are those who are persecuted because they do what God requires." (Matthew 5:10)

---

i   12- Steps reprinted with permission of Alcoholics Anonymous World Services, Inc. (AAWS).

ii   Eight Principles Based on the Beatitudes reprinted with permission of Zondervan.

STAYING THE COURSE/NO RELAPSE

My Shepherd, I praise You for all Scripture is inspired by You and is useful to teach me what is true and to make me realize what is wrong in my life. It corrects me when I am wrong and teaches me to do what is right. I praise You Father, as I use Your Word to prepare and equip me to do every good work. Father, You are my Rock; Your deeds are perfect. Everything You do is just and fair. Thank You Father, for being faithful, You do no wrong; how just and upright You are! Father, You were clothed in a robe dipped in blood, and Your name is the Word of God. I praise You as the Word became flesh and took a place among us for a time; and Your glory--such glory as is given to an only Son by His Father was seen in You--full of grace and truth.

Father, I don't worry about anything; but instead, I pray about everything. I tell You what I need, and thank You for all You do. I experience Your peace, which exceeds anything I can understand. Your peace will guard my heart and mind as I live in You, Jesus. One final thing, I fix my thoughts on what is true, honorable, right, pure, lovely, and admirable. I think about things that are excellent and worthy of praise. I keep putting into practice all I have learned and received from You—everything I heard from You and saw You doing, The God of Peace is with me.

Lord, help me to test everything I hear and say by Your standards and not mine. Search me, O God, and know my heart! Try me and know my thoughts! Help me to do a heart check daily, and turn over to You in prayer any hurts, exhaustion, anger, resentment, or tension. Lord, help me to speak Your Word to my life situations, and in doing so I know I am applying the healing hands of You, Jesus, directly to that pain. Help me to pray and read Your Word daily and guard this process as a holy quiet time. Lord, I humbly submit myself to You, and I resist the devil and he flees from me.

Lord, forgive me when I allow my mind to race with thoughts that are not of You. Forgive me when I do not humbly submit myself to You. Father, forgive me when I do not quickly arise from my pity pot. Forgive me when I think I must fight other's battles. Holy Spirit, bring to my mind those people, places and situations I need ask Your forgiveness: _____

_____ .

Lord, I forgive those who have been critical, unkind, or unappreciative. I forgive those who do not see the vision You have for me and hinder me in any way. Holy Spirit, bring to my mind those I need to forgive: _____

_____ .

Help me to not yield to temptation, but deliver me from the evil one.

A voice from behind cries, "This is the way." Follow it, whether it turns to the right or to the left. Be still, and know that I am God! You are honored by every nation. You are honored throughout the world. Lord of Heaven, Your armies are here among us; God is my fortress. In Jesus' name I pray! Amen![i]

---

i   Scriptural Reference: 2 Timothy 3:16-17 (NLT) Deuteronomy 32:4(NLT)Revelation 19:13 (NLT) Philippians 4:6-9 (NLT) John 1:14 (BBE) Psalm 139:23 (AMP), James 4:6-8 (NKJV) Isaiah 30:-21 (AMP & GW) Psalm 46:10-11 (NLT)

Reflections and Written Meditations

_____
_____
_____
_____
_____
_____
_____
_____
_____
_____
_____
_____
_____
_____
_____
_____
_____
_____
_____
_____
_____
_____
_____
_____
_____
_____
_____

STEP 11: We sought through prayer and meditation to improve our conscious contact with God, praying only for knowledge of His will for us and power to carry that out. [i]

PRINCIPLE 7: Reserve a daily time with God for self-examination, Bible reading, and prayers in order to know God and His will for my life and to gain the power to follow His will. [ii]

"Happy are those who are persecuted because they do what God requires." (Matthew 5:10)

i   12- Steps reprinted with permission of Alcoholics Anonymous World Services, Inc. (AAWS).

ii Eight Principles Based on the Beatitudes reprinted with permission of Zondervan.

GIVING THANKS AND PRAISE

Gracious Father, I lift Your name and praise You. I celebrate and thank You with my whole heart in the midst of the righteous and in the congregation. Your works are great and diligently sought out by me and I delight in them. Glorious Father, Your work is honorable and majestic and Your righteousness lasts forever. Thank You Father, for all of Your wonderful works to be remembered; You are gracious and full of compassion towards me.

Lord, I reverently seek You. You give me food and You always remember Your covenant with me. You have declared and shown me the power of Your works and have given me the inheritance of Your people. The works of Your hands are done with truth and justice. Your commandments for me are trustworthy. They last forever and ever. They are carried out with truth and decency. You, Lord, have sent salvation to me. You have ordered Your promise to continue forever. I proclaim Your name is holy, inspiring awe and fear. I have moral reverence for You, Lord, and this is the beginning of wisdom. Lord, I have good sense and follow Your commandments. My praise for You continues forever.

Lord, I am so grateful for the many healings and restorations You have laid before me. I will seek Your face and praise Your name all the days of my life. I will have a true reverence for You and fear Your name. I will admire all of Your glorious and wonderful creations. I will fear You at all times and grow wise by the renewing of my mind. I will cling to Your commandments and love You with all my heart and all my soul. I will love my neighbor as I love myself. I will be forgiving and charitable in all that You have provided. I will seek first Your Kingdom and its righteousness.

Father, forgive me when my actions do not show reverence and fear for You. Forgive me when I seek the easy way knowing full well I have bypassed Your way. Forgive me when I neglect to enter Your gates with thanksgiving and praise. Forgive me when my countenance is not reflective of Your victory over sin and the grave. Holy Spirit, bring to remembrance those people and places I need to ask Your forgiveness for:_____

_____ .

I forgive those who do not fear You and do not seek Your wisdom. I forgive those who do not recognize You as the provider of all things and the creator of all things. I forgive those who are solemn in their worship to You. I forgive those who complain continually and are ungrateful. Holy Spirit, bring to mind those people and places I need to forgive:_____

_____ .

Help me to not yield to temptation, but deliver me from the evil one.

Praise God, all You servants of His, you who reverence Him, both small and great! God is called The Word of God. From His mouth goes forth a sharp sword with which He can strike the nations; and He will shepherd and control them with a staff of iron. He will tread the winepress of the fierceness of the wrath and indignation of God the All-Ruler, the Almighty, the Omnipotent. On His robe and on His thigh He has a name inscribed, King of kings and Lord of lords. In the name above all names, Jesus, I pray, Amen![i]

---

i   Scriptural Reference: Psalm 111:1-10 , Revelation 19:5 , Revelation 19:13-16

Reflections and Written Meditations

_____
_____
_____
_____
_____
_____
_____
_____
_____
_____
_____
_____
_____
_____
_____
_____
_____
_____
_____
_____
_____
_____
_____
_____
_____
_____

STEP 11: We sought through prayer and meditation to improve our conscious contact with God, praying only for knowledge of His will for us and power to carry that out. [i]

PRINCIPLE 7: Reserve a daily time with God for self-examination, Bible reading, and prayers in order to know God and His will for my life and to gain the power to follow His will. [ii]

"Happy are those who are persecuted because they do what God requires." (Matthew 5:10)

---

i   12- Steps reprinted with permission of Alcoholics Anonymous World Services, Inc. (AAWS).

ii Eight Principles Based on the Beatitudes reprinted with permission of Zondervan.

GIVING BACK TO OTHERS

My Mentor, You gave me the example to follow by washing the disciples feet, for me to do to others. Father, You ask me who is the greatest, the one who sits at the table or the servant? You humbly replied that You are a servant among us and I thank You. Unselfish Father, You laid down Your life to set me free from every sin and to cleanse me so that I can be Your special daughter/son who is enthusiastic about doing good things.

Lord, You tell me that when I show brotherly love to people who are hurting, it is as if I have done it to You. I declare I will be a salt-of-the-earth person as You keep Your eye on me. I chose to walk according to Your will as You have chosen me to be on Your side. I will be a light, a reflection of Your goodness, and as a public city on a hill. I will let my light shine, being open and generous to others. Helping others to open up with You Lord, my generous Father in heaven.

Lord, help me to be a cheerful giver at all times, knowing I represent all that You have graciously given me. Empower me to hear Your small still voice and follow the direction You are leading me to give of myself. Give me boldness to profess the Good News wherever I go. Imbed in my heart the fulfillment of giving rather than receiving. Lead me to squash selfish-driven deeds under my feet.

Lord, forgive me when I put conditions on giving. Forgive me when I expect something in return, even if only recognition. Forgive me when I do not acknowledge the gift or the act of giving that has come from You. Forgive me when I hold back and feel that I must keep something in reserve for myself. Holy Spirit reveal to me those people and actions I need to ask forgiveness for:

_____ .

I forgive others who are driven by selfish desires. I forgive those who neglect to give as they have been given and recognize You Lord as the giver of all good things. Holy Spirit reveal to me those I need to forgive: _____

_____ .

Help me to not yield to temptation, but deliver me from the evil one.

Do not worship any other god; for the Lord, Whose name is Jealous, is a jealous (impassioned) God. All give praise and thanks to You, O God; Your wondrous works declare that Your Name is near and they who invoke Your Name rehearse Your wonders. In Jesus' name I pray, Amen![i]

---

i   Scriptural Reference: John 13:14-15 (GW) Luke 22:27 (GW) Titus 2:14 (GW) Matthew 25:40 (AMP) Psalm 101:6 (MSG) Matthew 5:14-16 (MSG) Exodus 34:14 (AMP) Psalm 75:1 (AMP)

_____

STEP 12: Having had a spiritual awakening as the result of these steps, we tried to carry this message to alcoholics (others), and to practice these principles in all our affairs. [i]

PRINCIPLE 8: Yield myself to God to be used to bring this Good News to others, both by my example and by my words. [ii]

"Happy are those who are persecuted because they do what God requires." (Matthew 5:10)

_____

i   12- Steps reprinted with permission of Alcoholics Anonymous World Services, Inc. (AAWS).

ii   Eight Principles Based on the Beatitudes reprinted with permission of Zondervan.

BEING A NARROW GATE RECRUITER

Blessed Father of sympathy, pity and mercy, You are the Source of every comfort, consolation and encouragement. I praise Your name because it is You who comforts me in every trouble, calamity and affliction, so that I may also be able to comfort those who are in any kind of trouble or distress, with the comfort with which I myself am comforted by You. I thank You Obedient Father, for the more I suffer for You, the more You shower me with comfort through Jesus. I praise Your name, Lord and Teacher, it is by Your humble example, having washed Your disciples feet, that You instruct me to wash other's feet.

Lord, I acknowledge and receive Your instruction and arouse the love which springs from a pure heart, a good clear conscience and sincere faith. As Your dear child, I will not just talk about love; but I will practice real love. As a prisoner for You, I declare I will lead a life worthy of the divine calling to which I have been called, with behavior that is a credit to the summons to Your service. I will live with complete humility and meekness, being unselfish, gentle, mild, and patient, bearing with others and making allowances because I love others. I will open my eyes so I can see what You show me of Your miraculous wonders.

Thank You Lord, for choosing me to be one of Your laborers. Continue to direct my steps and help me to make plans for my life that will glorify You. Help me Lord, to renew my mind and cling to the wisdom of Your Word. Strengthen me to do Your will and be receptive to Your calling by the Holy Spirit in my life. Lead me in Your Wisdom to glorify Your Kingdom. Open my ears that I may hear and my eyes that I may see Your marvelous works. Lift me up Lord, so I may have a word of encouragement for those You have placed in my path.

Father, forgive me when my actions do not exhibit the fruits You have given me. Forgive me for any missed opportunity to share Your Good News. Forgive me for not always having a servants heart. Forgive me when I neglect to humbly serve others. Forgive me for not being content to plant the seed, wanting to see only the harvest. Holy Spirit, bring to remembrance those people and places I need to ask Your forgiveness for: _____

_____ .

Merciful Father, I forgive those who do not seek Your Kingdom and its righteousness. I forgive those who are selfish and self-driven in their deeds. I will pray for and forgive those who do not readily accept the Good News. Holy Spirit, bring to mind those people and places I need to forgive: _____

_____ .

Help me to not yield to temptation, but deliver me from the evil one.

For everything there is a season, a time for every activity under heaven. God made everything beautiful for its own time. He has planted eternity in the human heart, but even so, people cannot see the whole scope of God's work from beginning to end. Whatever God does is final. Nothing can be added to it or taken from it. God's purpose is that people should fear him. What is happening now has happened before, and what will happen in the future has happened before, because God makes the same things happen over and over again. In Jesus' name I pray, Amen![i]

---

i   Scriptural Reference: 2 Corinthians 1:3-5 (AMP) 2 Corinthians 1:5 (NLT) John 13:14-15 (NLT) 1 Timothy 1:5 (AMP) 1 John 3:18 (MSG)
    Ephesians 4:1-2 (AMP) Psalm 119:18 (MSG), Ecclesiastes 3:1 (NLT), Ecclesiastes 3:11,14,15 (NLT)

Reflections and Written Meditations

_____
_____
_____
_____
_____
_____
_____
_____
_____
_____
_____
_____
_____
_____
_____
_____
_____
_____
_____
_____
_____
_____
_____
_____

STEP 12: Having had a spiritual awakening as the result of these steps, we tried to carry this message to alcoholics (others), and to practice these principles in all our affairs. [i]

PRINCIPLE 8: Yield myself to God to be used to bring this Good News to others, both by my example and by my words. [ii]

"Happy are those who are persecuted because they do what God requires." (Matthew 5:10)

---

[i]   12- Steps reprinted with permission of Alcoholics Anonymous World Services, Inc. (AAWS).

[ii]   Eight Principles Based on the Beatitudes reprinted with permission of Zondervan.

4 FLESH PRAYERS

Finally, my walk requires a daily battle with my flesh, that is, my sinful nature. I again returned to the Word to see what God had to say about my victory over anything that would try to rise up contrary to His Will for my life. Free will to choose was the defining factor for me, not only for life or death, but for whose will I would seek, mine or God's. This is where I learned I will fight the good fight, stay in the process, finish the race and always reach for the prize.

I had walked such a very long time in the world and had picked up many ungodly ways. I often would ask myself, how did I get so far from Holy. I would quickly learn that I was never farther from Holy than to reach out for His hand.

TAKING AUTHORITY OVER MY FLESH

God's SUPER (Holy Spirit) over my NATURAL (Flesh) = HOLINESS.

Supernatural: Of/ or relating to an order beyond the visible observable universe; of/or relating to God.

God is the supernatural creator and overseer of the universe. When Jesus ascended to heaven, He sent to me the Comforter, the Holy Spirit to dwell in me.i The Holy Spirit teaches, guides, comforts and intercedes for me.ii

The Holy Spirit came from above to lead me on this journey of enlightenment, entitlement and engagement of my natural, carnal self. He leads me to a victorious place of holiness in the name of Jesus (i.e. found in God's Will/Word), albeit a lifelong journey.

Flesh/carnal/human nature (the old man/woman): Pertaining to or characterized by the flesh or body, its passions and appetites, sensual; not spiritual, worldly.

The flesh is opposed to the Spirit, it refuses to place itself under the authority of God.

When I was living under the control of my old nature, I could not please God. Now being born from above by the Holy Spirit who lives in me, I trump over and subdue my carnal passions.iii

When my mother gave birth to me, it was the flesh of my mother and flesh of my father that produced my flesh, but the Spirit of God gives birth to my Spirit. I experienced my second birth by the Holy Spirit coming to live within me.iv

In the days of Noah, God said, His spirit shall not forever dwell and strive with man, for he also is flesh. God was so grieved in his heart because the wickedness of man was great in the earth, and that every imagination and intention of all human thinking was evil continually. God regretted creating man. God told Noah that he intended to put an end to all flesh, for through men the land is filled with violence.v I cannot imagine humankind on earth without the Holy Spirit to subdue the flesh--it must have looked like mayhem. How sad that God who created Adam to walk and talk with Him in the Garden of Eden is now grieved at His very creation. The Good News is that God's perfect redemptive plan of sending His Son, Jesus who reigns victorious over all sin, all flesh, all wickedness! You see, my flesh is nothing new to God.

God wanted me to seek His plan of action, His way, His will. I love what the prophet Isaiah said about repenting and seeking God's higher, holy ways. . .

Isaiah 55:6-9 (Darby) *⁶ Seek ye Jehovah while He may be found, call ye upon Him while He is near. ⁷ Let the wicked forsake his way, and the unrighteous man his thoughts; and let him return unto Jehovah, and He will have mercy upon him; and to our God, for He will abundantly pardon. ⁸ For My thoughts are not your thoughts, neither are your ways My ways, saith Jehovah. ⁹ For [as] the heavens are higher than the earth, so are My ways higher than your ways, and My thoughts than your thoughts.*

---

i   John 15:26 (Darby)

ii   John 14:26, Romans 8:14, 26 (Darby)

iii Romans 8:5-9 (GW)

iv John 3:5-7 (GW)

v   Genesis 6:3-7, 13 (AMP)

My God is willing to abundantly pardon me! I think how mercifully and abundantly He pardoned Paul, His beloved apostle.

Holy: Exalted or worthy of complete devotion as one perfect in goodness and righteousness. Holiness is the state of being holy.

I know there is only one sinless, unblemished lamb, JESUS, who was slain and is worthy of my complete devotion.i Unlike other creatures, I was made in the image of God and capable of reflecting His divine likeness.ii He calls to me to be holy, for He is holy!iii

Authority: Power to influence or command a thought, opinion, or behavior. Freedom granted by one in authority, a right.

I have been given authority in the name of JESUS, which is far above all rule and authority, power and dominion, every name, every title given in this age (this world), but also in the age to come (eternity).iv

To sum it up, I have been freed from the power of sin, I have become a servant to God, and my personal fruit is to do those things that lead to holiness, with the resultant life eternal.v God gave me a free will. My journey is filled with choices to make about whom I will serve. I had to ask the Holy Spirit first, to reveal to me my character distortions (carnal, flesh-driven ways), and then find out God's will for each. I could only find these revelations in the Truth of the Word of God, accompanied with the enlightening of the Holy Spirit. I had to come out of my ignorance, the old natural man, and learn what it meant to be holy.vi Just as the old testament temple had to be rebuilt, my temple is under reconstruction. Having no knowledge of God is a very dangerous domain of destruction for anybody (remember back there with Noah)--I could no longer reject God's will for my life.vii I now have arrived at a place of moral reverence (fear) for the Lord, and have a burning desire to understand and learn what is meant to be in communion with the Holy One!viii

I know deep in my heart this pursuit of holiness will be a life-long journey--one filled with many victories along the way. I had to ask the Holy Spirit (just as David did) to search me, know my heart, try me and know my thoughts. If there is any wicked way in me, lead me in the way of eternity (holiness).ix My final resting place, my eternity will be that beautiful garden as God intended it--Complete Holiness. Until that time, I have much work to do! Hence, I was led again to the Word to see what God had to say about my flesh.

The following "flesh prayers" are in no way meant to be complete, but rather those areas that my "old natural woman" has been enlightened to thus far.

---

i   Revelation 5:11-12 (NKJV)

ii   Genesis 5:1 (AMP)

iii   Leviticus 11:44, 19:2, 20:7 (AMP)

iv   Ephesians 1:21-22 (AMP)

v   Romans 6:22 (KJV)

vi   1 Peter 1:13-16 (NKJV)

vii   Hosea 4:1, 6 (NKJV)

viii   Proverbs 9:10 (NKJV)

ix   Psalm 139:22-24 (KJV)

Reflections and Written Meditations

Rebellion

My Ever-Present, Merciful Father, as Your servant, I have food and I have drink. I rejoice and sing out praises to You from the depths of the joy in my heart. In Your long-suffering, I am so thankful You called me by a new name and my former rebellion is remembered no more. Oh loving Father, You have been with me throughout my journeys like a cloud by day and a fire by night and I will obey Your commandments and follow Your plan. I abide in You and You graciously abide in me and have made Your home in me, by the Holy Spirit Whom You have given me. Abba Father, You are slow to anger and filled with unfailing love, forgiving me of every kind of sin and rebellion.

You disarmed the principalities and powers of my rebellion and made a bold display and public example of it. I stand triumphant over my rebellion in You, Jesus, by means of the cross. Jesus, I love Your name. You look upon me with mercy. You show me favor. I declare that only You establish my steps and direct me with Your Word. You do not let my iniquity have dominion over me. I confessed my rebellion to You and stopped trying to hide my guilt and You forgave me! All my guilt is gone! You were pierced for my rebellion, and beaten so I could be made whole. I declare You were counted among the rebels, and yet, bore my sins and interceded for my rebellion.

Lord, I will serve You all of my days. You have made me glad in redirecting, reinventing, and reviving that inner love, joy, peace and long-suffering as I trust and surrender to Your Will and Your Ways found in the Word. I thank You that even though labeled a rebel, it could not persuade You from Your journey to the cross. I too, will not be persuaded away from Your cross, Your cause, and Your call for restoration and salvation. You are the Final Authority. Lead me to recognize and submit to those You have placed in authority, being Your servant always to magnify You. Help me to always submit to the Your commandments, the laws of the land, rules and regulations set in place to guide me. Help me to have malice towards none.

Father, forgive me for any self-serving, self-justifying thoughts and manipulations to prove my righteousness. Forgive me for grumbling and being discontent for any situation or persecution that arises. Forgive me for not letting You be the final authority and vindicator. Forgive me for being stubborn, unyielding and calloused over matters of the heart. Holy Spirit show me those things I need to ask forgiveness for: _____

_____ .

Father, I forgive those who do not readily accept Your ways and Your truths. I forgive those so easily snared and caught up in the ways of the world. Holy Spirit, readily show me those I need to forgive: _____ .

Lord, Help me to not yield to temptation, but delivery me from the evil one.

Deep honor and bright glory to the King of All Time— One God, Immortal, Invisible, Ever and Always. Oh, yes! To the one and only God, our Savior through Jesus Christ, our Lord, be glory, majesty, might and dominion, power and authority, before all time and now and forever (unto all the ages of eternity). Amen! [i]

---

i   Scriptural Reference: Isaiah 65:13-17 (AMP) Exodus 40:38 (AMP) 1 John 3:24 (AMP) Numbers 14:18 (NLT) Colossians 2:15 (AMP) Psalm 119:132-133 (AMP) Psalm 32:5 (NLT) ! Isaiah 53:5,12 (NLT) 1 Timothy 1:17 (MSG) Jude 1:25 (AMP)

Reflections and Written Meditations

ANGER/BITTERNESS/WRATH

Compassionate Father of Peace, at one time I was living in the pleasures of my flesh, giving way to desires of my flesh and of my mind, and through Your great love for me, You made a way to save me by grace through Your Son, Jesus. I praise You as You richly fill every need I have in a glorious way through Your Son as well. Dear Father, indeed it was for my own peace that I had great bitterness, but You have lovingly delivered my soul from the pit of corruption, You have cast all my sins behind Your back. Gracious Father, it is not Your intention that I experience Your anger, but that I obtain salvation through my Lord, Jesus Christ.

I worship You in Spirit and rejoice in You, Lord. I have no confidence in my flesh. When I get angry, I will not sin. I will not let the sun set on my anger and give place to the devil. Rather, I will meditate within my heart on my bed, and be still. I declare I will get rid of all bitterness, rage, anger, harsh words, and slander, as well as all types of evil behavior. Instead, I will be kind to others, tenderhearted, compassionate, forgiving others, just as You have forgiven me. I choose to operate in the fruits of the Holy Spirit with love, joy, peace, patience, kindness, goodness, faithfulness, gentleness, and self-control. Against such things there is no law that can bring charge against me.

Lord, I trust you to uproot all of the deep seeded things in my heart that bring a tear to Your eye. I trust You to strengthen me to offer forgiveness for every painful deed and person who has hurt me. I trust You to direct my steps for this cleansing of my heart. I know Your strong right hand will be there to lift me up. I break and disconnect from the anger that has been passed on generationally to me and cut it off at its root. I am no longer held captive by unforgiveness. I will not let anger have a reflex-like effect on my behavior, nor feel the need for a quick rebuttal.

Lord, forgive me for becoming angry over trivial things. Forgive me for trying to control every situation and others. Forgive me Lord for assuming my way is the right way. Forgive me for placing unreasonable expectations on others. Forgive me for being self-righteous, hyper-critical, unhappy, judgmental, angry, and for having no thankfulness in my life. Holy Spirit show me those things I need to ask forgiveness for: _____

_____ .

Lord, I forgive others who have treated me harshly with words and actions out of anger. I pray for and forgive anyone who is holding a grudge. I forgive and show mercy to anybody who has offended me. I forgive others for being unhappy and bitter. Holy Spirit show me those people and circumstances that I need to forgive: _____

_____ .

Help me to not yield to temptation, but delivery me from the evil one.

There is no god who can compare with You—who can wipe the slate clean of guilt, turn a blind eye, and a deaf ear, to the past sins of Your purged and precious people? You do not nurse Your anger and You do not stay angry long, for mercy is Your specialty. That's what You love the most. In Jesus' name I pray, Amen! [i]

---

i   Scriptural Reference: Eph 2:3-5 (BBE) Philippians 4:19 (GW) Philippians 3:3 (NKJV) Isaiah 38:17 (NKJV) 1 Thessalonians 5:9 (GW) Ephesians 4:26-27 (NKJV) Psalm 4:4 (NKJV) Ephesians 4:31-32 (NLT) Galatians 5:22-23 (AMP) Micah 7:18 (MSG)

Reflections and Written Meditations

PRIDE/SELFISHNESS/EGOCENTRICITY

My Righteousness and Holy Father, I respect the fact that You do not play favorites. It is through Your Son Jesus, a gracious gift of unmerited favor and mercy, that I am justified and placed in right standing with You. I exalt You for passing over my former sins without punishment. Instead You chose to wash them with the blood of Your Only Begotten Son. This is Your proof in my present day that You alone are righteous, and You alone justify me by my true faith in Your Son, Jesus. You made the way for my pride and my boasting to be banished, not by my deeds, but by my faith in Him whom You sent. Merciful Father, You resist the proud, but give grace to the humble.

Lord, I declare I have turned from my self-indulgent, self-gratifying, prideful, boastful and malicious lifestyle that is worthy of death. I am counted as righteous not because of anything I have done or could do, but because of my faith in You, Jesus. Your joy lives in me, for my disobedience is forgiven and my sins are put out of sight. You keep no record of my sins. I proclaim not to be an empty soul being bloated with self-importance, but a person in right standing before You and with steady faith being fully alive through You, Jesus. I will have a humble spirit with the lowly and not accept any spoil from the proud. I will trust in the Lord and find goodness and be happy. I will put on the armor of light and walk properly. I will put on the Lord and make no provision for the flesh to fulfill its lusts. I will not act out on selfish ambition or be conceited. Instead, I will think of others being better than myself. I will not be concerned about my own interests, but rather I will be concerned with the interests of others. I will have the same attitude as Christ Jesus.

Lord, help me to always be humble and consider my over-inflated ability and wants of little regard. Lead me to seek Your kingdom and the needs of Your people first, trusting that You will meet every need when I do so. Father, Help me to not store treasures of things on earth, but rather to store up the treasures of things that are in heaven. Make my heart a treasure box of heavenly things. Fill me with a joy overflowing at the action of giving to others versus receiving for myself.

Forgive me for bragging and thinking that I have accomplished anything without Your guiding Light. Forgive me when I attempt to take matters into my own hands instead of releasing them to Yours. Forgive me for overlooking or ignoring the needs of others. Forgive me for trying to manipulate the Truth by putting eternal values on things of this world. Holy Spirit, show me the things I need to ask forgiveness for: _____

_____ ,

I forgive those who brag of their acumen, titles and achievements for self-glory and attention. I forgive anyone who thinks they are in any way better than others. I forgive those who try to put divisions or castes between myself and others. Holy Spirit, show me those I need to forgive: ___

_____ .

Help me to not yield to temptation, but delivery me from the evil one.

The Lord God Eternal says, "let not the wise boast in his wisdom; let not the mighty and powerful boast in his strength and power; let not the wealthy boast in his earthly riches. But let him who boasts give glory in this: that he understands and ***knows Me personally*** and recognizes My character, and that I am the Lord, Who practices loving-kindness, judgment, and righteousness in the earth. It is in these things that I delight." In the name of Jesus I pray, AMEN! [i]

---

i   Scriptural Reference: Romans 2:11 Romans 3:23-27 (AMP)Romans 4:5-8 (NLT) Habakkuk 2:4 (MSG) Romans 13:12-14 (NKJV)Matthew 6:19-21 (GW) James 4:6 (NKJV) Philippians 2:3-5 (GW) Matthew 6:33 (NKJV) Jeremiah 9:23-24 (AMP)

Reflections and Written Meditations

TONGUE/SPEECH PRAYER

Father My Master, I praise You as the fountain of life; It is in Your Light that I see light. Oh, compassionate Father, You continue Your loving-kindness towards me. You continue Your righteousness towards me as my heart is upright. Thank you Father, for You do not let the foot of pride overtake me, and do not let the hand of the wicked drive me away. Omnipotent Father, I praise You for by Your grace I am saved through faith; and not of myself: it is a gift from You, not by my works, so that I may not boast. I thank You, Father that no flesh will glory in Your presence.

Lord, I want to enjoy life and see good days, and I will keep my tongue free from evil and my lips from guile, treachery, and deceit. I declare and decree my tongue will be a wholesome tree of life, not perverse and a breach in Spirit. Death and life are in the power of my tongue, and I will choose to eat the fruit of it for life. I understand that I must be quick to listen, slow to speak, and slow to get angry. I will pursue those things which bring peace and which are good for everyone. When I discovered your words, I devoured them. They are my joy and my heart's delight, for I bear your name, Oh Lord God of Heaven's Armies.

Lord, help me to envision my tongue as a tree of life with roots, branches, and vines bringing forth Your words of life and life abundantly. Magnify my senses Lord, so my hearing will be keen and quick, while my speech will meditate on the tree of life. Bridle my feelings of displeasure in my circumstances so my anger will be of low regard. Lead me Holy Spirit, in words of edification only. Reign in my perceived need to respond to unkind words or actions. Help me to cut off and abandon any knee jerk reactions to wrongdoing or perceived wrongdoing.

Lord, forgive me for putting conditions on forgiveness. Forgive me Lord, when I am quick to anger and respond with my words. Forgive me when I allow my mind to spin over situations and put up walls of inaccessibility. Forgive me for any sarcasm with underlying meanings. Forgive me when I put up barriers that hamper the reflecting of Your glory. Holy Spirit reveal to me those things I need to ask Your forgiveness for: _____

_____ .

Lord, I forgive those closest to me for speaking words of condemnation. I forgive those who complain and grumble over seemingly trivial things. Lord, I forgive those who for the sake of not knowing You, speak words of death. Holy Spirit, reveal to me those who I need to forgive: _____

_____ .

Help me to not yield to temptation, but delivery me from the evil one.

Jesus sits at God's right hand and His enemies are made a footstool. From Your mouth goes forth a sharp sword with which He will smite, afflict and strike the nations; and He will shepherd and control them with a staff of iron. as He is God, the All-Ruler, the Almighty, the Omnipotent. On His robe and His thigh, a name inscribed, KING OF KINGS, LORD OF LORDS. In the Blessed name of Jesus, I declare and decree with confidence my petitions. Amen! [i]

---

i   Scriptural Reference: Psalm 36:9-11 (AMP) Ephesians 2:8-9 (KJV) 1 Peter 3:10 (AMP) 1 Corinthians 1:29 (NKJV) Proverbs 15:4 (KJV) Proverbs 18:21 (AMP) James 1:19 (NLT) Romans 14:19 (GW) Jeremiah 15:16 (AMP) Revelation 19:15-16(AMP) Matt 22:44 (MSG)

Reflections and Written Meditations

GLUTTONY PRAYER

Father My Victory You created me in Your own image; the image of You. You did form my inward parts; You knit me together in my mother's womb. Thank You for making me so wonderfully complex! Your workmanship is marvelous—how well I know it. Father, You are the one who brought me out of the womb, the one who made me feel safe at my mother's breasts. I was placed in Your care from birth. I praise You Father, for You have permanently imprinted a picture of me on Your palms; my walls are being rebuilt continually in Your sight. I praise You for I have not received a spirit that makes me a fearful slave. Instead, I have received Your Spirit when You adopted me as Your own child. Now I call You, "Abba, Father."

Lord, I believe that just because something is technically legal doesn't mean that it's spiritually appropriate. If I went around doing whatever I thought I could get by with, I'd be a slave to my whims. I know the old saying, "First you eat to live, and then you live to eat?" Well, it is true that the body is only a temporary thing, but that's no excuse for me stuffing it with food, or indulging it with sex. Since You, Lord honored me with a body, I will honor You with my body! I will pattern my life after Yours, and learn from those who follow Your example. My conduct will show that I am not an enemy of the cross of Christ, and therefore, not bringing tears to Your eyes. My god is not my appetite, and I will not brag about shameful things. I will not think only of life here on earth. I am a citizen of heaven, where You live Lord, and I eagerly await for Your return as my Savior. It is You who will take my weak mortal body and change it into a glorious body like Your own, using the same power with which You will bring everything under Your control.

Help me to be disciplined in spirit, not giving way to any notion of a right to over-indulge. Lead me to pray over everything I consume. Discipline me to do that which is unpleasing to me for the ultimate benefit to my body, soul and spirit. I decide now to trust You, God, and by Your strength conform to Your will, trusting Your supernatural power at all times. Lead me to fast, making a commitment, and documenting my course, staying focused on my goal. I know that I have been called to live in freedom. I will not use my freedom to satisfy my sinful nature or my body. Instead, I will use my freedom to serve others in love.

Lord, forgive me when I bring a tear to Your eye for my wasteful consumption at self-driven feasts. Forgive me for recollecting, revisiting, and elevating those feasts pleasing to my palate, but not to my body, Your temple. Forgive me when I use food or drink to comfort any emotional pain or loss, thereby, not trusting You whole-heartedly. Forgive me for not acknowledging You in prayer for anything I consume. Forgive me for not seeking fair portions for my sustenance, while neglecting those living without any form of nourishment. Forgive me for not fasting and praying and waiting on You. Holy Spirit, bring to mind those things I need to ask Your forgiveness for: _____.

Lord, I forgive society and the media for the enticements to over-indulge in all manners of consumption. I forgive the companies, suppliers and manufactures for promoting unhealthy choices for my temple for reasons of greed. I forgive those companies who taint Your provisions with chemicals and things deleterious to my health. I forgive anybody who seeks a relationship with me centered around over-indulgence of food or drink. Holy Spirit bring to mind those I need to forgive: _____.

Help me to not yield to temptation, but delivery me from the evil one.

To everyone who is victorious, He will give some of the manna that has been hidden away in heaven. He will give to each one a white stone, and on the stone will be engraved a new name that no one understands except the one who receives it. In Jesus' name I pray, AMEN. [i]

---

i   Scriptural Reference: Genesis 1:27 (NLT) Psalm 139:13-14 (AMP/NLT) Psalm 22:9-10 (GW) Isaiah 49:16 (AMP) Romans 8:15 (NLT) 1 Corinthians 6:12-13 (MSG) Philippians 3:17-21 (NLT) Galatians 5:13 (NLT) Psalm 133:1-3 (AMP) Revelation 2:17 (NLT)

Reflections and Written Meditations

SEXUAL IMPURITY

Abba Father My Owner, I praise You for keeping me awake, watchful and prayerful, so that I may not be tempted by my flesh; for my Spirit indeed is willing, but my flesh is weak. Thank You Father for sending the Holy Spirit to me who puts to death the evil deeds prompted by my flesh, and I shall live forever. I thank You that a I am led by Your Spirit and am Your daughter/son. Precious Father, Your will for me is to live a pure life and keep away from sexual promiscuity. You teach me to appreciate and give dignity to my body, not abusing it, as is so common among those who know nothing of You.

Lord, I will always exercise and discipline myself, deadening my carnal affections, bodily appetites, and worldly desires, seeking in all respects to have a clear and blameless conscience, devoid of offense towards You and towards others. I declare that the craving for sensual gratification, greedy longings in my mind, false assurance in my own resources or earthly things, do not come from You, Lord, but instead are of the world. The world will pass away along with all these forbidden cravings, passionate desires, and lusts, but I will do Your will and carry out Your purposes, and I will live forever. I declare, I will honor You with my body and run from sexual sin! I abstain from sexual immorality knowing that my body is the Temple of the Holy Spirit.

Lord, I know that sexual and lustful temptations have been in existence since the fall of Adam and are nothing new. Lead me to recognize and learn from Your Word, these snares and landmines the enemy tries to set. Gently show me the grave consequences of the sacrifice of my body to satisfy my own flesh. Then quicken me to seek the Holy Spirit who dwells in me to cast down these vain imaginations. I will put to death all of the old lusts including all sexual misuse (adultery, sex outside of marriage, homosexuality, bestiality, incest, pornography, prostitution and any form of sexual misconduct).

Forgive me Lord, when I seek acceptance and approval from others through sexual intimacy. Forgive me for thinking I am entitled to act on my feelings. Forgive me Lord, for accessing those places, literature, electronic media, and entertainment venues that promote sexual self-gratification and impropriety. Forgive me for looking at others and lusting for them in my heart. Lord, forgive me for thinking I can compromise Your principles. Forgive me Lord, for the consequences affecting others by my poor choices to serve my selfish lusts and desires. Holy Spirit, reveal to me those things I need to ask your forgiveness for: _____

_____ _.

Lord, help me to forgive others who have been active participants in my sexual impropriety. I forgive those who have been controlling and manipulating. I forgive those who claim if it feels good do it. Lord, show me any situation, act or person I need to forgive: _____

_____ .

Help me to not yield to temptation, but deliver me from the evil one.

God's throne is in His temple where He rests His feet. His people will no longer dishonor His holy name by acting like prostitutes and doing disgusting things, and He will live among them forever. God has spoken what is good and what He requires of His people; that is to do what is right, to love mercy, and to live humbly with Him. God's voice cries out to the city: The fear of My name is wisdom. All assembled in the city must listen. In Jesus' name I pray, AMEN! [i]

---

i   Scriptural reference: Matthew 26:41 (AMP) Romans 8:13-14 (AMP) 1 Thessalonians 4:3-5 (MSG) Acts 24:16 (AMP) 1 John 2:16-17 (AMP)
    1 Corinthians 6:18-20 Ezekiel 43:7-9 (GW) (NLT) Micah 6:8-9 (GW)

Reflections and Written Meditations

FLESH CARDS

This leads to the interactive/personalized section known as... "FLESH CARDS." These are personalized wallet-sized cards or 3 x 5 cards in your own handwriting describing who God is, and who you are in Christ Jesus, and the scripture you will carry to stand on daily. These scriptures can be taken from the prayers, or your own personal fortified scripture from the Bible. Keep these cards where you know a temptation of the flesh will be made against you (i.e. drawer in kitchen, your desk at work, by your computer, on the dash of your car, your wallet, etc.).

You are getting the connection between real life then and real life now. God has never changed. He is the same yesterday, today and forever. Heaven and earth will pass away, but His Word will never pass away. Speak it into your personal life and experience the power!

FLESH CARD COMPONENTS:

Who God is (see page 14)
Who I am in Christ (see page 15)
My knowledge/victory verse related to this challenge! These are just a few of the names of God and Jesus, and who I am in Christ. Have some fun and find your own in the Bible!
SPEAK IT OUT LOUD AS OFTEN AS NECESSARY and MAKE AS MANY CARDS AS NECESSARY!

EXAMPLES:

REBELLION

My Ever-Present God of Truth and Faithfulness, I am Your Chosen and You call me by a new name. I have turned from my rebellion and am now Your servant. You remember my rebellion no more.

(Isaiah 65:13-17)

ANGER/WRATH

Jehovah Eternal, I am Near to You and set apart. When I become angry, I will not sin, but rather I will rest (taking a spiritual time-out) and be silent. I will sacrifice my right to speak and trust in Your Eternal existence.

(Psalm 4:3-5)

SELFISH PRIDE

Lord God My Righteousness, I am One in Christ. I do not live in strife and self-conceit, but in humility of mind and humbleness of mind in my activities of daily living. I will not be concerned with only my interests, but I will exalt the best interests of others.

(Philippians 2:3-4)

TONGUE/SPEECH

My Master, My Owner, I am Complete in You. I am trusted to spread the Good News, as I speak not to please men, but to please You. You are continually searching my heart and testing my motives.

(1 Thessalonians 2:4)

OWN IT--Speak God's Truths--MAKE IT
(make your personal flesh cards)

Who God is (see page 14); Who I am in Christ (see page 15); My victory verse related to this challenge!

SPEAK OUT LOUD OFTEN, MAKE COPIES OF CARDS, PLACE CARDS STRATEGICALLY

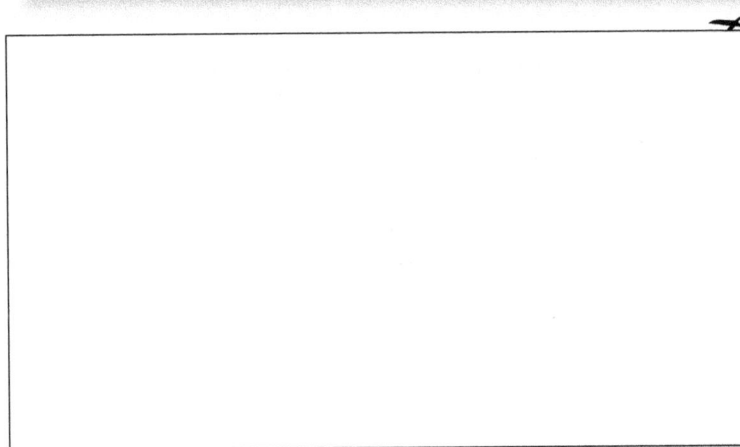

CURSING

My Ever-Present God, I am a Light of the World and declare my words will be a wholesome tree of life, not perverse and a breach in Spirit.

(Pr. 15:4)

TEMPTATION TO DRINK:

God My Victory, I am an Overcomer and I conduct myself honorably in the open of daylight, not in reveling and drunkenness.
(Rom. 13:13)

SEXUAL IMPURITY

My Master, My Owner, I am Your Child. I will not sin against my own body but run from sexual sin. My body is the Sanctuary of the Holy Spirit. I do not belong to myself, but have been bought with a high price, and will honor You with my body.

(1 Cor 6:18-20)

OWN IT--Speak God's Truths--MAKE IT
(make your personal flesh cards)

Who God is (see page 14); Who I am in Christ (see page 15); My victory verse related to this challenge!

SPEAK OUT LOUD OFTEN, MAKE COPIES OF CARDS, PLACE CARDS STRATEGICALLY

ANXIETY/FEAR:

God My Peace, I am a New Creature, and You have not given me a spirit of fear, but of power, love and a sound mind. (2 Tim 1:7)

God My Peace, My Comforter, as a Citizen in Your kingdom, I have inherited Your peace and my heart will not be troubled or fearful about any circumstance or situation I am facing. (John 14:27)

VENGEANCE

God My Righteousness, I am Confirmed Blameless, and do not need to get even with anybody, as I know You will take care of it. I will conquer evil by doing good.

(Rom. 12:19,21)

ROAD RAGE

Lord God My Peace, I am Your Friend, and it is possible for me to live in peace with everybody on these roads.

Lord bless that driver and keep him safe on his journey.

(Rom. 12:18)

OWN IT--Speak God's Truths--MAKE IT
(make your personal flesh cards)

Who God is (see page 14); Who I am in Christ (see page 15); My victory verse related to this challenge!

SPEAK OUT LOUD OFTEN, MAKE COPIES OF CARDS, PLACE CARDS STRATEGICALLY

5 PERSONAL TESTIMONY

Please allow me to begin my personal testimony with this disturbing definition of human trafficking, a term I myself did not become familiar with until my late 40's. This is where I began to face my giant!

WHAT IS HUMAN TRAFFICKING?

As defined by the United Nations Office on Drugs and Crime.

Article 3, paragraph (a) of the Protocol to Prevent, Suppress and Punish Trafficking in Persons defines Trafficking in Persons as the recruitment, transportation, transfer, harboring or receipt of persons, by means of the threat or use of force or other forms of coercion, of abduction, of fraud, of deception, of the abuse of power or of a position of vulnerability or of the giving or receiving of payments or benefits to achieve the consent of a person having control over another person, for the purpose of exploitation. Exploitation shall include, at a minimum, the exploitation of the prostitution of others or other forms of sexual exploitation, forced labor or services, slavery or practices similar to slavery, servitude or the removal of organs.

MY STORY IS NOT ONE OF WHAT WAS DONE TO ME, BUT WHAT WAS DONE FOR ME.

I was born in Wayne, Michigan, a suburb of Detroit. I had two brothers who were five and seven years older than me. My neighborhood was mostly boys and pretty close-knit. I was also known as the miracle baby, as my mother who was Rh-negative had four miscarriages before my birth. Being the only girl in my family and the "miracle baby," I was pretty spoiled. I had cousins who lived two houses down, who were older than me except for the youngest boy, Jeff. My Uncle Jack spoiled me too. You could say I was used to getting my way from a very early age.

My mother's father, Papaw Wilson, was a coal miner converted Pentecostal Minister, but "got religion" when my mother was in high school—so her goal was to get out of the house right after graduating. She was forced to quit playing basketball because they wore shorts. My father was raised in a Catholic home, went to Catholic school, and says he was pretty much beaten into submission by the nun's. He was referred to as the black sheep or the bad boy. My parents did not attend church, except when visiting Papaw. Papaw was affectionately known as Sweet William by his parishioners. My mother would leave my father in his alcoholic rages and flee to stay with her family, but always return for the sake of the children. My father's sisters, my aunts, would call my mom a saint for staying with my dad. I remember going to my Papaw's church on these occasions, and singing Do—Lord, Oh Do—Lord, Oh Do remember me, Oh Lordy in four-part harmony with my cousins as little children at the front of the church. The Lord showed me much later in life that my parents did truly love each other and that my mother was the only person who genuinely had shown my father unconditional Agape love. My father loved Reverend and Mrs. Wilson, as he referred to my grandparents, and it is through the prayers of my mother and her family that I know my father was saved.

While my parents did not go to church, I went to Calvary Baptist Church with a neighbor, Vi Holt (who had 2 sons) from about the age of 5 until 12 and was water baptized at the age of 12. Then Vi moved away and I no longer went to church. I am sure it was a goal of Vi's to see me baptized before she moved. She gave my mother a very old doll called a Miss Chase doll, to "put up for me," which I will refer to later. Vi passed away a few years ago and I often think of her fondly, for setting the groundwork for me to know Jesus as my Lord and Savior.

I was a tomboy, played baseball with all the neighborhood boys from sun up to sun down—pretty special being the only girl's door they would knock on and ask if Sheila could come out and play ball—always picked first or a team captain. It was a sort of "sand lot" ritual to play ball from sun up to sun down in the summer, often into the darkness playing a game we called "which way did it go." I remember telling myself as a child, "I AM NEVER GETTING MARRIED AND NEVER DRINKING!"

We were what you would call the average post WWII middle American family—The house, the car, the wife, the kids, the alcoholic veteran. At the age of 15, I found myself plotting and planning ways to get out of my house, being rebellious, and doing drugs and skipping school. I had become the prodigal daughter. My older brothers had left home defiantly and confrontationally with conflicting relationships with my dad. You see all of us children were defenders of our mother, resenting our father for his cruelty and abuse of her while drunk. At 15, such a tender age, transitioning from junior high to high school was not an easy transition for me. I no longer captured the attention from the neighborhood boys by my athletic ability. I went from being a straight-A student athlete to failing every class--skipping school, smoking pot/hashish, doing mescaline and THC daily. I began to sell them to support my own use--sports of no interest, quit volleyball,-- quit basketball--

getting high, covering my pain and loneliness. I ran away from home for no other reason than to get away. I went to stay with the drug dealers, who I only knew as people to get high with, "casual, friendly business acquaintances," or so I thought. Being high played an important part in the distortion of the true nature and intent of those around me. We partied for a few days and then some strangers came over—strangers to me, but apparently not to them. You see, the dealers needed me gone—I was an accident or bust waiting to happen. I was jail-bait, an under-age, truant minor, and definitely good for a harboring or kidnapping charge, or an even greater threat for a raid. So they did the most frugal thing they could think of, they sold me to their friends. I was told in secret by a woman who lived in this house that I had been sold to these so-called "friends." I had no idea what she was talking about. "Sold, you can't sell people," I told myself. I would later reflect on how she was trying to tell me to flee without getting caught herself. You see these friends were, the "big ballers" so to speak . They were members of a motorcycle gang called the "Huns of Detroit." Fear would begin to set in as I was forcefully removed from this house, shortly after she told me this.

"THE HUNS" as they call themselves, take their name from Attila the Hun, 409 AD, and boast in their history how Attila went out to pillage towns, snatch young women for sexual pleasure, and cause mayhem and devastation, and that Attila the Hun is their honored hero.

I was taken to their clubhouse --a cinderblock building with no windows and bars over the only entry door. Inside there was a dark and seedy big room with 2 pool tables, a bar, tables and chairs, and a juke box. Two smaller rooms were to the left. My naivete for what was about to take place was evident by my abounding fear. For 2 nights and 2 days I was bound to a bed and raped by various gang members. I was not a very cooperative participant as I remember crying "kill me, kill me—I just want to die" and would attempt to fight at various times while being held against my will—the athlete in me surfaced and I instinctively fought back. I was beaten and drugged. I recall when being led back into this room, there was a cork bulletin board where ladies panties were pinned with thumb tacks; their sort of sick, demented trophy case—yet, still in my youth as to the ways of the world, this did not register with me until again much later.

The third night, the party was over, I was taken out on a country road with another man they called a "probie;" he was a biker on probation for initiation into the gang. He had been severely beaten with pool cues, something I visually saw, and was bloody, drugged and drunk and unable to stand or walk. I am sure me watching this near-death beating was intentional on their part. We were both dumped on the roadside like stray dogs in the county, in the dark. He kept pleading with me to help him up, but oh no, no way--he was one of them. Beaten, raped and sobbing, I began to run. I walked, and ran, and walked and walked and walked and got to a paved road and hitchhiked, something I had become fearless at with girlfriends of mine when we would skip school and get high. An elderly man had picked me up, and I asked him to please take me home that I was very ill. He must have been an angel—he drove me home and never questioned me or spoke. I did not even have bearings or knowledge of where I was. GOD'S EVER PRESENCE IN MY BLINDNESS BROUGHT THE PRODIGAL HOME.

I remember telling myself that I had seen more evil in this one weekend than I ever knew existed in the world. I attribute this experience to my easy recognition and acceptance of Satan reigning here on earth, which would come from Bible teachings much later in my adult life. It was something I never questioned because I had experienced and seen first-hand the evil one.

1 Peter 5:8 (Darby) *Be vigilant, watch. Your adversary the devil as a roaring lion walks about seeking whom he may devour.*

I would remain in silence for many years after these events, as the gang members told me that they knew where I lived and if I told anybody about what happened they would kill not only me, but my family as well. From the violence I had seen and experienced that weekend—I took their threats very seriously. My silence and isolation served to form many walls. I know today that traffickers use force, fraud, and/or coercion to maintain control over their victims to engage them in illegal activities.

I had been gone about 10 days. I came home a wreck, a recluse, and thinking and seeking ways to get my revenge. Not to mention being physically ill. My mother took me to the doctor and I stood in silence with him also. I don't remember going back to my high school in Wayne. There is a time period that I have no recollection of. I trust God for the remembrance of all things that will bring Him glory.

My parents had been working and building a retirement home in a small northern town in Gladwin, MI. My father took an early retirement, and we moved to the country. I am sure my drug seeking lifestyle weighed heavy on this early retirement; a sacrifice, my adolescent mind would see as torture. I was the City Mouse now having to be the Country Mouse. I hated it. I would sun in my bikini in the yard in the summer. I smoked and would take the tractor out for joy rides on the oilfield roads behind our house. Our neighbors would call my father and report my dangerous antics. I was a menace to our neighbor's quiet country life.

Then at my new high school of 300 students, the athlete resurfaced—basketball star, 20 points a game, and touring the state playing women's softball in the summer. Yet, smoking on school grounds and sneaking into the bars on the weekends with a fake ID, only to be caught by my coach.

In a creative writing class, I would attempt to tell my story through a homework assignment. I wrote my story with a twisted ending and received an A, but was shut down by my teacher's comments that my story was "Likely to scare the heck out of some young girl, but not very believable." This only served to confirm in my adolescent mind that silence was the best route.

I graduated from high school, but struggled with college, going from college to college, from relationship to relationship—always ending with a big breakup and then it was time to split again. This behavior deepened my bondage to be in control, to avoid conflict at all costs, and if that were not possible to cover it up with drugs and alcohol. I found the best way to face my giant, was to split!

My thoughts of revenge—learning to use dynamite and blow up their clubhouse while they were engaged in a weekend frenzy, were slowly fading. GOD'S EVER PRESENCE IN MY BLINDNESS because vengeance was His and not mine. I would likely not be telling you my story today if I had gone through with my plan of revenge.

Control and covering up my secret would be a constant that would perpetuate my drug and alcohol use, anger and bitterness. My self-esteem was so low, but I was still a fighter.

At the age of 21, I had moved back to a suburb of Detroit, called St. Clair Shores. My brother lived about an hour away from me, and one night after visiting him, going out drinking, we went to Denny's for breakfast; you know, the bar-closing ritual in an effort for the party not to end. While sitting at the table, a man with long red hair and a long red beard came up to my brother and said, "Hey, Duncan, what's happening?" Of all my perpetrators, this would be only one of maybe two I would recognize because he looked like one of those yard leprechauns or gnomes--short and stubby, long red hair and a long red beard. I asked my brother if he was a biker, and he said "yes." It was then, six years after my rape, that I told a family member. YET AGAIN, GOD'S EVER PRESENCE IN MY BLINDNESS. Who knows what horrendous crimes could have occurred if my brother would have known about my rape when it happened.

In 1981, I moved to Houston at the prodding of my cousin. There was an automobile industry recession in Michigan and even though I was working, I was ready for a change. She assured me I could get a job at Cameron Iron Works, which I did. Now I was really a real City/Country mouse.

Party, party every night and dancing at the Roxy, while working at Cameron Iron Works in Capital Purchasing. Always had a job, always had money, always had a boy-friend, always in CONTROL—but really OUT OF CONTROL! I dated a bartender at the Roxy, a civil engineer student, who would later become my husband.

During this relationship, I became pregnant—IMPOSSIBLE--both of us had assured each other we could not have children—no medical documentation for this, mind you, just our individual summations for not having had children already from our sexual promiscuity. His solution was for me to get an abortion, but remember, I was in control and that was not acceptable for me—my body, my baby. So again, I would have it done my way. It was my way or the highway. I told him he could leave and did not have to be involved if he chose not to, and I would have the child myself. I win again, or so I thought. He now wanted to get married, being so moved by me wanting to keep his child—so we did. A child, what was I thinking--maybe this was the unconditional love and acceptance I so longed for.

He was a Muslim from Iran and I thought he was the nicest man I had ever met. Religion played no part in my choice for a husband—all emotional, sensational, romantic feelings. Again, much later in my adult life I would learn the scripture. . . 2 Corinthians 6:14 (NKJV) *Do not be unequally yoked together with unbelievers. For what fellowship has righteousness with lawlessness? And what communion has light with darkness?*

My husband was an absentee parent in the home, always working, or what I would later find out to be always playing and supporting mistresses—something from his culture I am sure was acceptable and permitted. Working full time with 3 children, I had little time to babysit him. I was quick to defend him when people would come with stories and proof—also known as DENIAL.

Five years into my marriage, two Baptist preachers came and knocked on my door and invited me to church. I was ready for a change—a change in heart, a change in activities, and looking to meet new people other than those at work and home. God planted me for eight years at Almeda Baptist Church, where I made some life-long friends, and began my study of the scripture--one of my favorite things. While I hated history in high school, I loved learning about all the travels and miracles in Jesus' time and before. Also, this began my eight years of sobriety and deliverance from alcohol, cigarettes and social cocaine use. My Muslim husband would accept Christ and be baptized in the baptismal at our church—a really big miracle at this little Baptist church, as you can imagine. This picture sits on my son's desk today, but Satan doesn't waste much time; the accuser of the brethren was hard at work. I am reminded of how Satan came immediately after Jesus was baptized and tempted him. My husband did not become planted in God's Word or in church and sold his convenience store and became involved in the adult entertainment industry—sex, crack cocaine and near death.

My plea to him was how could you sell the business without consulting me and by the mere fact that you have a daughter, I was disgusted and horrified by his decision to go into this business—Satan, who I have heard called the evil genius, used the very same abuse I suffered at the hands of sexual exploitation, to bring an end to a 14-year marriage in 1996.

1 Timothy 6:10 (AMP) *For the love of money is a root of all evil; it is through this craving that some have been led astray and have wandered from the faith and pierced themselves through with many acute [mental] pangs.*

While going through the divorce process I came on hard financial times. I also sensed a feeling of rejection from my church family for my failed marriage and the shame for his business choices. My Miss Chase doll from my Sunday school teacher, Vi Holt, brought in a whopping $500—GOD'S EVER PRESENCE IN MY BLINDNESS, and another house payment met.

Conversations with my ex-husband were based on Acts 10:15-16, where Peter had the vision for the salvation of the Gentiles when God spoke to him three times stating:

Acts 10:15-16 (NKJV) [15] *And a voice spoke to him again the second time, "What God has cleansed you must not call common." [16] This was done three times. And the object was taken up into heaven again.*

I told my ex-husband that every woman in these clubs is somebody's daughter, but most importantly they were daughters of the Most High Almighty God. They are cleansed by Christ's blood and not common, not dirty, and not unworthy of love and dignity, and His saving grace.

Following my divorce, I would again take control and that same control would be what the enemy would use to lead me away from church and God. I had convinced myself that I was not the kind of person who wanted to live alone. My heart's desire was to marry again.

Psalm 37:4 (AMP) *Delight yourself in the Lord, and He will give you the desires of your heart.*

But, I did not delight in the Lord and let Him give me the desires of my heart. Instead, I returned to the old way of doing things, my controlling way, my plan instead of God's plan. My will instead of God's will.

Proverbs 9:10 (GW) [10] *The fear (moral reverence) of the Lord is the beginning of wisdom. The knowledge of the Holy One is understanding.*

My lack of moral reverence, to be morally pleasing to God led me down a slippery slope of backsliding. I lacked wisdom and fear of the Lord. This led me into the heart and hands of an alcoholic, again my choice, not God's, but what a big heart and hands, and a sense of humor as big as Texas. Alongside him, the athlete resurfaced in a softball game, as well as some other old ways or often referred to as the "old man" or in my case the "old woman." A familiar calling from a happier day when asked, "can Sheila come out and play ball."

2 Corinthians 5:17 (NLT) *This means that anyone who belongs to Christ has become a new person. The old life is gone; a new life has begun!*

Hence, my backsliding journey begins. On my 39th Birthday while watching my new friend play ball, we celebrated with pitchers of beer. My saying of "3 beers in 8 years" would come to a screeching halt. So would my other saying I often repeated to my children, "don't drink beer, beer is bad." While it was a slow, slippery course, it was still a road that would lead to destruction, alienation from my family, my church and most importantly, God.

We got married in November, 1997, and blended 2 families. He with 1 daughter, and me with 1 daughter and 2 sons. While I had always told my children that beer is bad, don't drink beer, I found myself trying to be a closet drinker. While I fooled only my children for a few years, my public drinking became common place. What was a weekend celebration became an almost nightly indulgence while playing softball four nights a week. Competition became the newest member of the family. Everything I did was clothed in competition and distrust. I was now bitter, judgmental and hypocritical.

Finally, after 10 years of marriage, I realized that I would not be able to stop drinking with my husband in the house, so I asked him to leave. This was my lowest point, morally washed out, separated from God, bitter and angry. It would be this separation that would be the start of God's destination for me.

I still loved my husband, but could no longer function in my out of control lifestyle. I desperately needed to get some order and my joy back. God made a way for us to attend the Celebrate Recovery program at Lakewood Church. We attended while separated for 4 months, and then were reunited, and completed our yearlong CR Program. God rapidly restored our marriage, reuniting us as 1, instead of the 2 separate people we had always been.

Once I turned my will over to God's will for my life, what I call "rapid restoration" came rolling my way. I praise His name for the victories and challenges that come and are yet to come, knowing and trusting He only wants good for me and my family.

Satan wanted to devalue, destroy my body, my temple, but instead of being sold for a high price, I have been bought and ransomed for a much higher price.

1 Corinthians 6:19-20 (MSG) *19 Or didn't you realize that your body is a sacred place, the place of the Holy Spirit? Don't you see that you can't live however you please, squandering what God paid such a high price for? The physical part of you is not some piece of property belonging to the spiritual part of you. 20 God owns the whole works. So let people see God in and through your body.*

The Lord has shown me that I was plucked from a life of abuse and sexual exploitation at the hands of the enemy—the so-called trafficker and that was Satan's plan for me.

In Genesis 50:20, we hear what Joseph said to his brothers as he forgave them for selling him into slavery. . . Genesis 50:20 (AMP 20) *As for you, you thought evil against me, but God meant it for good, to bring about that many people should be kept alive, as they are this day.*

But God's Ever Presence In My Blindness

I was a fighter and God had a place for me in His army, and it took me a mere 35 years to see the battle was not mine, but His. Yes, 35 years ago near my own back yard, a human trafficking story. Hard to believe—not really. But why is it so hard for us to see the epidemic state this abomination to God has reached today. Or is it just merely that we don't want to see it?

A genocide was thwarted for the Jews in Persia, when Mordecai sent a message to Esther...an orphan called to the palace of a king to be his queen. . .

Esther 4:14 (AMP) *14 For if you keep silent at this time, relief and deliverance shall arise for the Jews from elsewhere, but you and your father's house will perish. And who knows but that you have come to the kingdom for such a time as this and for this very occasion?*

Esther fearlessly became the hands, the feet, and the voice for God, to speak out for others whose cries could not be heard.

*GOD IS NOT THROUGH WITH MY STORY,
BUT I AM SO THANKFUL THAT HE IS
THE AUTHOR AND FINISHER OF MY FAITH.*

I pray that the fighter in us all will rise up to the calling of that perfect place, that perfect will in the Lord's army.

Reflections

Reflections

Reflections

Reflections

Credit and Thanks

- Most importantly to God for His Master-full plan of sending His Son, Jesus for my reconciliation with Him, and for His Word found in the Bible.

- To Jesus, for being such an obedient Son and example throughout His earthly journey.

- To the Holy Spirit, who intercedes for me continually and directs my plans and steps.

- To my husband, Jose Rivera, who walked with me into recovery and now walks in unison with me in oneness in our Christ-centered marriage.

- To my children, Sarah, Joseph, Kristin and Abraham for their loving kindness.

- To the recovery newcomer, who allows me to hear their pain and witness their victories in Jesus.

- To the body of Christ at Lakewood Church, who graciously opened their doors to me.

- For two "hopeless alcoholics," Bill W. and Dr. Bob, who brought hope to millions post prohibition through sobriety and serenity, and developed the 12-steps to sobriety.

- To the authors and creators of Celebrate Recovery (CR), Pastor John Baker and Pastor Rick Warren.

- To my local Lakewood Church CR family and leaders, Pastors John and Shirley Molina.

- To my sponsor, Minister Verenda Hodge.

- To Pastors Suzette and Kirbyjon Caldwell for their work at The Prayer Institute and Windsor Village United Methodist Church and their commitment to Kingdom Building.

- To Anita Carman, for her selfless commitment to the advancement of women in ministry through Inspire Women.

- To Roy Urrego for patiently working with me on the book design, re-design, visitation, and re-visitation.

- To Cheri Brown, for editing and proofing.

MODERN DAY SLAVERY

- Out of 21 million forced labor and sex victims worldwide, around 4.5 million were trafficked.
  –International Labor Organization

- 1 in 5 victims of human trafficking will travel through Texas along the I-10 corridor.
  –Department of Justice

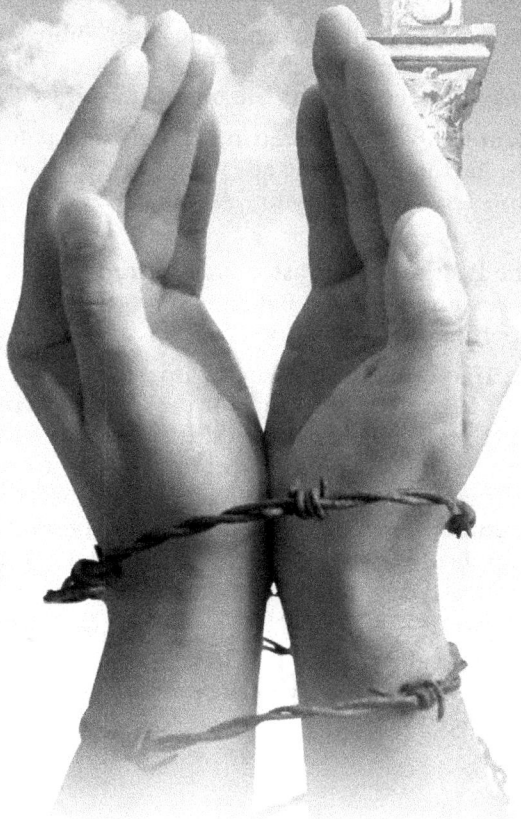

REFERENCES

- "Scripture quotations taken from the Amplified® Bible, Copyright © 1954, 1958, 1962, 1964, 1965, 1987 by The Lockman Foundation. Used by permission. Copyright info: www.Lockman. org."

- ESV Copyright and Permissions Information The Holy Bible, English Standard Version® (ESV®) Copyright © 2001 by Crossway, a publishing ministry of Good News Publishers.All rights reserved.ESV Text Edition: 2007

- "Scripture is taken from GOD'S WORD®. Copyright 1995 God's Word to the Nations. Used by permission of Baker Publishing Group. All rights reserved." (www.godswordtranslation.org)

- 'Scriptures and additional materials quoted are from the Good News Bible © 1994 published by the Bible Societies/HarperCollins Publishers Ltd UK, Good News Bible © American Bible Society 1966, 1971, 1976, 1992. Used with permission.'

- "Scripture taken from The Message. Copyright 1993, 1994, 1995, 1996, 2000, 2001, 2002. Used by permission of NavPress Publishing Group. See www.messagebible.com."

- Scripture quotations marked (MOFF) are from The Bible: James Moffatt Translation, Copyright © 1922, 1924, 1925, 1926, 1935 Harper Collins, San Francisco, CA, Copyright © 1950, 1952, 1953, 1954, James A. R. Moffatt.

- "Scripture taken from the New King James Version. Copyright © 1982 by Thomas Nelson, Inc. Used by permission. All rights reserved. See www.thomasnelson.com."

- "Scripture quotations marked NLT are taken from the Holy Bible, New Living Translation, copyright 1996, 2004, 2007. Used by permission of Tyndale House Publishers, Inc., Wheaton, Illinois 60189. All rights reserved. See www.tyndale.com/faq.asp?id=7."

- "Scripture quotations marked "TLB" or "The Living Bible" are taken from The Living Bible [computer file] / Kenneth N. Taylor. electronic ed. Wheaton : Tyndale House, 1997, c1971 by Tyndale House Publishers, Inc. Used by permission. All rights reserved. See www.judeministries. org/copyrights.php."

- Eight Principles Based on the Beatitudes by Pastor Rick Warren taken from Celebrate Recovery, A Purpose Driven Recovery Resource by John Baker, Foreword by Zondervan, Copyright 1998, 2005, Zondervan. Used by permission of Zondervan. See www.zondervan.com.

- The Twelve Steps and Twelve Traditions are reprinted with permission of Alcoholics Anonymous World Services, Inc. ("AAWS"). Permission to reprint the Twelve Steps and Twelve Traditions does not mean that AAWS has reviewed or approved the contents of this publication, or that A.A. necessarily agrees with the views expressed herein. A.A. is a program of recovery from alcoholism only - use of the Twelve Steps and Twelve Traditions in connection with programs and activities which are patterned after A.A., but which address other problems, or in any other non-A.A. context, does not imply otherwise. Additionally, while A.A. is a spiritual program, A.A. is not a religious program. Thus, A.A. is not affiliated or allied with any sect, denomination, or specific religious belief.

- *Praying to Change Your Life,* by Pastor Suzette T. Caldwell, copyright 2009 - Suzette T. Caldwell, Destiny Image Publishing, Inc. Reproduced by permission of Destiny Image Publishing, Inc.

We want to hear from you.
Please send your comments
about this book to us in care of:
rivera.sheila@sbcglobal.net

Thank you.

The Author

PRAYERS

FOR RECONCILIATION, RECOVERY AND RESTORATION

A Personal Journey For Reconciliation With God Through The Holy Spirit By The Spoken Word

MIND OF CHRIST

Jehovah Eternal, I am Near to You and set apart. I will be transformed by the renewing of my mind with Your Holy Word by:

Reading Daily
Exercising Meditation
Now Believing
Earnestly Applying
Willfully Obeying

(Romans 12:2)

Then he said, *"I tell you the truth, you will all see heaven open and the angels of God going up and down on the Son of Man, the one who is the stairway between heaven and earth."*

–John 1:51 (NLT)

From the Author **Sheila Rivera**
(More Inside)

"I was jail-bait, an under-age, truant minor, and definitely good for a harboring or kidnapping charge, or an even greater threat for a raid. So they did the most frugal thing they could think of, they sold me to their friends. I was told in secret by a woman who lived in this house that I had been sold to these so-called "friends." I had no idea what she was talking about. 'Sold, you can't sell people,' I told myself. I would later reflect on how she was trying to tell me to flee without getting caught herself. You see these friends were, the 'big ballers' so to speak. They were members of a motorcycle gang called 'The Huns of Detroit'.

"A deep, dark secret for many years would be the lie that would keep me bound and interfere with my relationship with God. The veil removed, the Light turned on, and the accuser cast down. God's ever-presence in my blindness would be my victory cry while exercising my spiritual vision and now discerning good and evil."

Narrow Gate Recruiter Books
ISBN-13: 978-0615661353
ISBN-10: 0615661351

BISAC: Self-Help/Twelve-Step Programs

ISBN 061566135-1

www.ingramcontent.com/pod-product-compliance
Lightning Source LLC
Chambersburg PA
CBHW081634040426
42449CB00014B/3299